BRANSON

COUNTRY THEMES AND NEON DREAMS

BRANSON
COUNTRY THEMES AND NEON DREAMS

LELAND AND CRYSTAL PAYTON

PHOTOGRAPHS BY LELAND PAYTON

WITH ADDITIONAL HISTORIC PHOTOGRAPHS BY

G.E. HALL, VANCE RANDOLPH, TOWNSEND GODSEY AND OTHERS

ANDERSON PUBLISHING, INC.   BRANSON, MISSOURI

DEDICATION

To Homer Wadsworth who wisely advised us to keep the faith.

Half title page. At the western end of 76 Country Boulevard stood "Jim Lane's Cabin," built in the late 1800s by Mathias Corvin Shearer, who was said to have been the model for the Jim Lane character in Harold Bell Wright's novel, *The Shepherd of the Hills.* His daughter, Grace, was also thought by some to be the model for the novel's heroine, Sammy Lane.

Verso. Audience at Echo Hollow Amphitheater in Silver Dollar City.

Title page. 1. Vance Randolph photograph from the 1940s of Taney County musicians. (Lyons Memorial Library, College of the Ozarks)

2. The bright lights of Branson's 76 Country Boulevard, looking west.

Below. Vance Randolph photograph, 1930s (Lyons Memorial Library, College of the Ozarks)

Left. Downtown, or Old Branson, seen from across Lake Taneycomo atop Mount Branson.

Contents page. The Grand Palace before a matinee.

Published 1993. First Edition
Published by Anderson Publishing, Inc.
P.O. Box 357, Branson, MO 65616

Library of Congress Catalog Card Number 93-073535
ISBN 0-9636666-2-2

Design and composition by Jim Hawkins
Typesetters on Olive Street
Printed in Singapore

CONTENTS

Very serpentine in its course, the river carried us toward every point of the compass in the course of the day; sometimes rocks skirted one shore, sometimes the other, never both at the same place, but rock and alluvion generally alternating from one side to the other, the bluffs being much variegated in their exterior form, extent and relative position, giving perpetual novelty to the scenery, which ever excited fresh interest and renewed gratification, so that we saw the sun sink gradually in the west without being tired of viewing the mingled beauty, grandeur, barrenness, and fertility, as displayed by the earth, rocks, air, water, light, trees, sky and animated nature; they form the ever winding, diversified and enchanting banks of the White River.

— *Henry Rowe Schoolcraft*, JOURNAL OF A TOUR INTO THE INTERIOR OF MISSOURI AND ARKANSAS IN 1818 AND 1819.

THE LIFE IN A DAY AT BRANSON

Scenery, or what is beautiful about landscape, is subjective. There are, however, some places that nearly everyone thinks are worth viewing. Paintings, photographs, and poems are made about such scenery. Travelers flock to see it. Before the music, before the comedy, before the theme parks and motels and restaurants, there were the rugged, rocky, oak and hickory forested hills of the Ozarks. Through them ran sparkling clear creeks, tributaries of the mighty White River. This scenery was appreciated by the earliest explorers and settlers as much as it is by today's visitors. Modified though it is by reservoirs and roads and other works of man, the landscape still exhibits a wild and seductive beauty.

Pointe Royale Village and Country Club, a private residential development and golf course, below the scenic overlook on Highway 165. Table Rock Dam is on the left in the distance.

In the distance, beyond Pointe Royale, lies 76 Country Boulevard.

7

Branson lies between two dams on the White River, Powersite and Table Rock. Table Rock Dam, several miles upstream from Branson, was built by the U.S. Army Corps of Engineers in the late 1950s. It created a very deep lake with 745 miles of shoreline. Downstream about 18 river miles is Powersite Dam. Built by the Ozark Power and Water Company and closed in 1913, it created Lake Taneycomo (named for Taney County, Missouri). At that time, it was one of the largest artificial impoundments in the U.S., although by today's standards it is scarcely more than a long pool in the river.

The water used to generate electricity at Table Rock Dam comes from depths of 110 to 115 feet, creating water temperatures of 45 to 50 degrees in Lake Taneycomo – too cold for native fish, but ideal for trout. Today, a trout hatchery stocks Taneycomo mostly with rainbows and a few browns. Table Rock Lake, on the other hand, is a warm water fishery with white bass, crappie, bluegill, channel cat, and – the object of tournament fishing – largemouth bass.

Sunset at State Park Marina, Table Rock Lake.

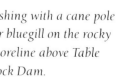

Fishing with a cane pole for bluegill on the rocky shoreline above Table Rock Dam.

Three rainbow trout taken from the public fishing dock on Lake Taneycomo at Rockaway Beach.

School children tour The Shepherd of the Hills Trout Hatchery located immediately below Table Rock Dam.

All of Branson's theme parks provide fun, food, and lots to do. Shepherd of the Hills, Silver Dollar City, and Mutton Hollow use local history themes. The Shepherd of the Hills Homestead is the actual site of many of the events in Harold Bell Wright's 1907 novel. Mutton Hollow, also a setting in the novel, is today an 1890s crafts and entertainment village as well as home to the Wright Museum. Silver Dollar City's foundations were those of Marmaros, a late 19th century mining town laid out around the entrance to Marvel Cave. Some of the original buildings at Silver Dollar City are authentic old structures moved from the White River bottoms to make way for Table Rock Lake.

White Water, as its name implies, is a water park. You have to get wet to do White Water, where the decorative motif is distinctly Polynesian.

Wave pool at White Water.

The Great American Plunge at Silver Dollar City.

Clydesdales at The Shepherd of the Hills Homestead pull wagons full of tourists up to Inspiration Tower. More adventurous visitors can ride a horse on a trail ride over "the trail that is nobody knows how old."

1930s merry-go-round in the County Fair area of Mutton Hollow.

It's a bus . . . it's a boat . . . it's a duck! Branson is home to one of the largest flocks of vintage amphibious assault vehicles in the country. Now brightly painted and on a peaceable mission, they assault the traffic on 76 and the beaches and waters of Table Rock Lake.

Pink and powder blue chenille bedspreads no longer flap in the breeze along 76 Country Boulevard. Outstanding opportunities to acquire the most trendy (as well as old standard) yard ornaments still exist, but not in the immediate environs of multi-million dollar developments. Hillbilly motif novelties, alas, are now in short supply, having fallen prey to

The souvenir stands may not be as resplendent today as they were in the 1950s, '60s, and '70s, but eye-grabbing theaters, restaurants, motels, and fun-things-to-do places are in inflorescence. The new garden of roadside delights has not completely pushed the old flowers out either. Right among the latest plantings of tourist attractions and accommodations are some choice examples of earlier styles. Roadside Branson is old, new, and in between.

With its phantasmagoria of miniature golf courses, boat-shaped restaurants, symbolic signs, metaphorical signs, signs with bold and literal lettering announcing gas, food, lodging, souvenirs, fireworks, and—that most uncommon of contemporary travel experiences—live entertainment, the Branson roadside glows in the dark of the rocky oak and hickory hills. The pot of gold this neon rainbow leads to may be only a smile, but millions of people think it's worth the journey.

changing tastes. But then, the good old days didn't offer hand painted sawblades or mailboxes air-brushed with today's popular residential roadside icons like Guernsey cows or largemouth bass. Take heart, seekers of bygone touristware, the multitude of flea markets and antique malls still provides opportunities to acquire souvenirs of vacations past.

The hills may have been drilled by road cuts and the rivers partially tamed by dams, but the flow of the Anglo language runs unrestrained through the hills and halls of Branson. After the Branson roadside, the country music theaters offer a cool, dark space to experience a music older than the highway cuts and dams.

Plucked and bowed strings and the emotion-charged human voice singing of love and pain, joy and despair, of God, country and the simple pleasures of rural existence have always been and remain at the core of Branson's music.

The Brumley Music Show at 76 Music Hall.

One of Branson's earliest shows, The Presleys' Mountain Music Jubilee. The stage set is no longer a barn interior, but the music is as solidly country as it has always been.

Carlotta Gail, singing at
Campbell's Ozark Country
Jubilee, is a long-time
Branson favorite.

The Baldknobbers have been performing
in the Branson area since 1959.

June Carter Cash, like her
husband Johnny, brings an
international reputation as a
country singer to Branson.

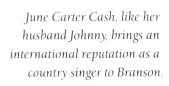

Shoji Tabuchi's entrance is outlined by a sunburst of ruby red laser light.

Today the sounds of brass and woodwinds can be heard echoing from the walls of the new music shows.

Many Branson shows feature a full complement of bass players and drummers and are now adding choreographers to their staffs. Dorothy Tabuchi has put a Broadway spin on Shoji's show.

The themes of country music may be as old as the hills, but the lighting, sound systems, costumes, and presentations are evolving into a distinctive art form on the Branson stage. The foundation of country music, and, indeed, much of American popular music, is the English ballad, a song that tells a story. Nothing in this tradition, however, rules out million-dollar sound systems, computer-controlled stage lighting or comfortable seats in air-conditioned auditoriums.

Arriving in a flying saucer from the planet Vegas, Wayne Newton greets his audience.

The central idea of a Branson music show is to have a good time. Like the music, Branson's comedy is tried and true and red, white, and blue. Americans have always been noted for an exuberant and physical sense of humor. The skits and bits in the shows are the same down-to-earth material that amused frontier audiences. Like Mark Twain and Will Rogers, these outrageous Branson storytellers can tap our funny bones in such a precise way that laughter becomes irrepressible.

*Atmosphere is his job —
Wayne Milnes plays Mike the
Mechanical Man at 76 Music Hall.*

*"Pump Boys and Dinettes." New shows are
bringing new sources of comedy to town.
This new style is still rooted in old-
fashioned American humor.*

*Then there's the matter of Jim Stafford.
Like Ray Stevens, his comic genius is
deeply southern and individualistic.*

Below. *Droopy Drawers, played by Jim Mabe.*
Right. *Herkimer, played by Gary Presley.*

Some folks may think they are too sophisticated for hillbilly humor. Such people have not been in the audience of a Branson country music show. In these two cases, the comics are founding members of Branson's two pioneering shows. It's rare in history for the court jester to own the castle.

Branson has become such an extraordinary recreation and entertainment capital that it no longer needs "Missouri" to complete its name. Fewer and fewer people ask, as Frank Sinatra supposedly asked Wayne Newton, "How can I come, when I can't find it on a map?"

Branson has been inaccurately described as a hillbilly Vegas, the new Nashville, and even Planet Branson. In fact, it not only has a longer history than most vacation/recreation attractions, but it also has its own look and way of doing things.

The Branson Mall has more than groceries and a Wal-Mart. It features nearly continuous live music in the skylit court.

Bungee jumps are everywhere, but from this one you can see some of the most unusual signage in the country.

Kenny does Elvis to an appreciative audience.

22

Adjacent to The Grand Palace, the Grand Village's specialty shops surround brick courtyards, fountains, plazas, and an occasional juggler.

"Ray's 56," a Ford Sunliner, sports an airbrushed picture of The Grand Palace on its wheelcover.

Even those who work so long and hard to build and maintain the Branson boom can find a moment to reflect, to kick up their heels, or to swap some "tell-me-where-you're-from, I'll-tell-you-where-I'm-from" stories.

From Inspiration Point, where Harold Bell Wright pitched a tent and wrote *The Shepherd of the Hills* in the early 1900s, to Taneycomo lakefront in Old Branson is a distance of less than five miles as the crow flies. The landscape is steep, however, falling about 500 feet, and every winding road, clear creek, and foggy valley in between is steeped in history. Neon-lined 76 Country Boulevard began as a trail from Branson's and Hollister's hotels and train depot to the cabins of The Shepherd of the Hills Farmstead and Marvel Cave. For almost 90 years vacationers have been coming to this "Shepherd of the Hills Country" looking for and finding experiences and entertainments unavailable back home.

A spirited square dance occurs during intermission at The Shepherd of the Hills Theatre. The audience can mix with the cast as the fiddlers compete with tree frogs and cicadas. The play itself is a piece of history. The tempo of the barn dance, where you can spin around with the beautiful girl who plays Sammy Lane, moves with the heartbeat of the moment.

At Shadow Rock Park, site of the old county seat before Bull Shoals Lake was built, the Taney County Riding Club holds a hard-riding rodeo every June. The Swan Creek bottom dirt thrown up by the hooves of the cowgirl's horse or hit hard by unsuccessful bronc- and bull-riders, is no illusion. The rocks and trees and creeks are real. So is the country culture that still permeates these White River hills. Savor a bit of that local reality along with the shows.

THE WHITE RIVER WILDS

No record survives of what native American Indians called it, but the French named it Riviere Blanche, the White River. As it meandered, it cut into the uplifted grey limestone formed in the basin of very ancient seas. Never glaciated and standing above water longer than any other geographic province of the U.S., the Ozarks has resisted the plow, the road, and the rapid changes that characterize more accessible and more populous regions of America. Stone and Taney counties lie in the heart of the wild White River country, about as far upstream as steamboats could travel. After the railroad crossed the White at Branson, generations of tourists came, first to hunt and fish in one of the last strongholds of Ozark wilderness, then to relax in a healthy outdoor environment, and now to experience the pleasures and surprises of America's musical and entertainment traditions.

The Ozark landscape is deeply river cut. Some, but by no means all, of its clear spring-fed rivers have been dammed to make lakes which, not surprisingly, are also clear. Due to the suppression of wildfires started by lightning and abetted by Indians and early settlers to keep the savanna of the plateaus and hilltops open for game and livestock, the Ozarks today may have more trees than it once did. The first white explorers rode across huge open prairies that today are nearly impenetrable brushy woods. Of course, the huge, centuries-old giants of the virgin pine and hardwood forests of the steep slopes and bottoms are gone, cut for lumber and railroad ties in the late 1800s and early 1900s. Still, all in all, the Ozarks has resisted the kind of change our civilization has wrought where agriculture and urbanization have prospered. Many areas are still semi-wilderness, and nowhere have the native flora and fauna been subdued completely.

It's not remarkable, then, that those who came to live in the Ozarks valued this kind of wild landscape and developed a lifestyle, which, while not immune to change, does resist the wholesale reordering of place and personality that characterizes industrial America. Hillbillies still live in these hills.

White River valley, circa 1915

There are not many real Americans left now, and we do not understand them any more. The Ozark hill-billy is a genuine American—that is why he seems so alien to most tourists. In a sense it is true that the American people are making their last stand in the wilderness, and it is here, if anywhere, that we must go to meet our contemporary ancestors in the flesh.

– *Vance Randolph*, THE OZARKS, AN AMERICAN SURVIVAL OF PRIMITIVE SOCIETY, *1931*

One of Vance Randolph's sources of Ozark folksongs, circa 1935. (Lyons Memorial Library, College of the Ozarks)

The Appalachians, and later the Ozarks, were settled by fierce, freedom-loving Celts from Scotland, Ireland, and Wales, and yeoman English. They brought with them a music that expressed both life's pleasures and life's pains. Along with their love of music they brought a tradition of outrageous story-telling and authority-mocking humor.

You can still hear the echo of this passionate music and bodacious humor in the numerous country music shows in Branson. It was here 150 years ago. It will be here 150 years from now. The fiddles and guitars are plugged in now, the girls may wear spangled spandex instead of calico or buckskin, and the target of satire is a current politician rather than King George III, but the voice of the Celtic/hillbilly soul is irrepressible. Hard times didn't dim it, nor will prosperity affect its essentials: a love of natural beauty, a keen wit that mocks pomp and pretense, and a nearly fanatical need to express in song and story life as it is most deeply felt and lived. As you gaze across the fog-filled Ozark valleys, recall the sad and haunting way a country fiddle pierces the silence, leading to the moment when a country singer fills the room with a sad yet beautifully told story of the mixed fate of those who dare to love.

While few, if any, Ozark natives wish to return to the primitive conditions of life as it was lived in the not-too-distant-past, most are proud of their heritage. Like log cabins, wood-burning stoves, and muzzle-loading rifles, the outhouse is a symbol of this pioneer heritage. It's also a source of humor in many of the country shows. The memory of "the little house out back" seems destined to be preserved in Ozark folklore long after outhouses themselves are all but gone.

"Jim Lane's Cabin," taken around 1914 by G.E. Hall. The photographer and his family stand in front of what they called "this famous old cabin." (Lyons Memorial Library, College of the Ozarks)

Above. "You will see the natives all along the highways weaving baskets. This is a very pleasant as well as profitable work, as they sell enough to the tourists, or 'furners' as they say, to help them live a 'right smart while.' The baskets are made in various shapes and sizes, and mostly of white oak."
— Pearl Spurlock in OVER THE OLD OZARK TRAILS, 1939. Vance Randolph photograph from the 1920s. (Lyons Memorial Library, College of the Ozarks)

Walker Powell runs the steam- and foot-powered lathes at Silver Dollar City. Walker's grandfather, Truman Powell, was said to have been Harold Bell Wright's model for The Old Shepherd. Truman Powell was vice president of the Marble Cave Manufacturing Co. in 1884. Renamed "Marvel Cave" in the 1920s, this landmark was the primary tourist attraction before Silver Dollar City grew up around it in the 1960s.

"Marble Cave, Stone Co., MO. April 16, 1909. Made by G.E. Hall, Notch, MO." (Lyons Memorial Library, College of the Ozarks)

Only a few miles from the theaters, the upper reaches of Roark Creek still provide a boy and his dog a place to go and things to do.

Gigging from a john boat. The clear waters of White River tributaries allow hillfolk the opportunity to harvest suckers, an abundant native fish that does not normally succumb to hook and line fishing. Vance Randolph photograph from 1928. (Lyons Memorial Library, College of the Ozarks)

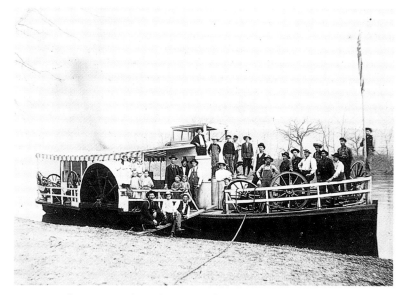

Steamboating on the White River for all practical purposes ended at old Forsyth, where the shoals became too fast and rocky.

Essential to Branson's success is the quality of its waters, remarked upon from the earliest days of exploration and noticed today by even the most casual visitor. The Ozarks is a karst region, an uplifted limestone plateau penetrated by sinkholes, caves, and springs. There is widespread local recognition of the value of its clear, pure water and the need to protect this remarkable resource.

Coolin' off in Roark Creek a short distance from where it skirts the north edge of downtown Branson.

Lake Taneycomo gave paddlewheelers on the White River a new lease on life. Today's visitor can take a leisurely dinner cruise, complete with live music, along the lake's 22-mile length.

Shoving our canoe into the stream, [we] found ourselves, with a little exertion of paddles, flowing at the rate of from three to four miles per hour down one of the most beautiful and enchanting rivers which discharge their waters into the Mississippi. To a width and a depth which entitles it to be classified as a river of the third magnitude in western America, it unites a current which possesses the purity of crystal, with a smooth and gentle flow, and the most imposing of delightful scenery . . . Every pebble, rock, fish, or floating body, either animate or inanimate, which occupies the bottom of the stream, is seen while passing over it with the most perfect accuracy; and our canoe often seemed as if suspended in the air, such is the remarkable transparency of the water.

— *Henry Rowe Schoolcraft*
JOURNAL OF A TOUR INTO THE INTERIOR
OF MISSOURI AND ARKANSAS IN 1818 AND 1819.

Swan Creek near Forsyth, where it
empties into Bull Shoals Lake.

◀ *Piped spring on
the campus of the
College of the Ozarks.*

COMPTON. FERRY   BRANSON MO
352 HALL PHOTO CO

*Compton Ferry
on the White River
at Branson*

The White River Line, which connected Branson to the larger world in 1905, began passenger service in 1906. Built by the St. Louis and Iron Mountain Railroad, it merged with the Missouri Pacific in 1917. Soon after the publication of Harold Bell Wright's SHEPHERD OF THE HILLS in 1907, intrigued tourists began arriving in the Branson area.

With improved highways and Americans' love of the family car, passenger service to Branson declined as it did elsewhere. There is currently no train service into Branson, but in the summer of 1993 Branson Scenic Railway initiated tours from Branson to Bergman, Arkansas, and Reeds Spring, Missouri, along the historic White River route.

WHAT HAROLD BELL WRIGHT AND THE RAILROAD WROUGHT

At the close of the 19th century it became apparent that the American frontier would soon be only a memory. The war cries of Indians could be heard only in traveling Wild West shows. Gone were the vast herds of buffalo. Gold couldn't simply be picked up as placer out of a stream bed; it had to be mined. Plows had cut into the virgin tallgrass prairie. Men with axes and cross-cut saws were chipping away at the dark forests that only a few decades earlier had seemed infinite and eternal. Game, for the first time, became scarce. Some of the wildest creatures, like elk, bear, mountain lion, timber wolf, and eagle, had all but disappeared from the Ozarks.

We paid a price for our prosperity. America's headlong rush to industrial might had pushed any semblance of the frontier back into inaccessible regions like the Ozarks, and this progress had also begun to punish the very people who had been part of the earliest pattern of settlement, the old Anglo-Celtic pioneers. Reflective men like Harold Bell Wright sought out pockets of wilderness to savor the frontier experience before it disappeared. On his first trip in 1896 he found not only a wild and beautiful country along the James and White Rivers in Stone and Taney Counties, Missouri, but also a proud and independent group of settlers, whose personalities and lifestyles provided the inspiration for his novel, *The Shepherd of the Hills*. As well as being a hunter and fisherman who sought out relatively unspoiled sporting opportunities, Harold Bell Wright was a minister who cared about people, even people who were at the time unfashionable.

THE SHEPHERD OF THE HILLS *has been made into four movies. The earlier versions, scripted by Wright himself, are truest to the novel.*

Those who faced an uncertain future in the new, transformed America were his favorite subject matter. Hillfolk, cowboys, and Native Americans were romantically but sympathetically depicted in many of Wright's books.

When Wright began *The Shepherd of the Hills* in 1903, Branson was little more than a post office. No dams had yet been built on the White River. The rails that eventually brought so many of the changes that doomed the frontier and would banish some of its colorful cast had not yet been laid. At the end of the novel that began Branson's long history as a tourist destination, the old shepherd reflects on the railroad's role in effecting change:

> Rising to his feet and pointing to Roark valley, the old shepherd said, "Before many years a railroad will find its way yonder. Then many will come, and the beautiful hills that have been my strength and peace will become the haunt of careless idlers and a place of revelry. I am glad that I shall not be here."

HAROLD BELL WRIGHT

Harold Bell Wright achieved wealth and fame from the sale of his books and the movies made of them. His childhood, however, was difficult. His father, William A. Wright, had returned from the Civil War with medals, souvenirs, and troubled memories. The experience led him to strong drink and prevented him from holding jobs. Wright's mother, Alma T. Watson Wright, whom he loved dearly, died when he was 11. He and his three brothers never had a stable home again.

Will Wright sent the boys to live with different friends and relatives, periodically reappearing in their lives, but never able to keep the family together.

After years of uncertain living arrangements, itinerant jobs, and some college education, Harold Bell Wright found that his way with words and sympathetic concern for ordinary people made him a captivating speaker. He felt his calling as a minister, although without feeling the need to join a particular

Harold Bell Wright memorabilia is on display at the Harold Bell Wright Museum and Theater in Mutton Hollow. Wright's last living son, Norman, who established the museum, had a long career at Disney Studios. He designed the installation and scripted and produced the film on his father's career shown at the museum.

Left. *The original manuscript, in Wright's own hand, of* THE SHEPHERD OF THE HILLS.

Above left. *Wright loved to work with his hands. He was not only a painter, but also an accomplished craftsman, working with wrought iron and wood. The observational skills he learned as a painter contributed to the excellent descriptions of landscape and physical settings in his novels.*

Above 2nd left. *Wright's own painting of "the trail that is nobody knows how old."*

Above 3rd left. *Civil War memorabilia belonging to William A. Wright, Harold's father.*

denomination. His first full-time ministry was at Pierce City, Missouri. Thirty-five miles southeast of this prairie town lay the still relatively wild and unsettled hills of the White River. Wright first began exploring that area and becoming acquainted with its inhabitants about 1896.

In the hills he formed a lasting friendship with the remarkable Levi Morrill, an acquaintance of Longfellow and Hawthorne who had worked as a newspaperman in New York

 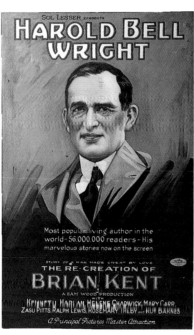

under Horace Greeley, and founder of newspapers in Denver, Galveston, and some small towns in Kansas. Another Ozark friend was Truman Powell, who had worked with Morrill at one of his Kansas newspapers before founding a newspaper in Galena, county seat of Stone County. Powell had homesteaded in Fall Creek and then became vice president of the company that attempted to mine Marble Cave (with limited success for bat guano, but no other minerals).

Although Wright acknowledged only that "Uncle Ike" in his book was directly modeled after Levi Morrill, as time went on the inhabitants of the region became convinced that all the characters represented actual members of the community. Some even began to go by the names of their *Shepherd of the Hills* characters. The truth of the matter is that while the plot

was completely Wright's, it seems probable that he did draw heavily on his acquaintance with the settlers of Stone and Taney counties in constructing the vivid personalities that populate his novel.

Throughout his life Harold Bell Wright was plagued by respiratory illness, severe enough to interrupt his work for long periods and cause him to seek out healthful climes like the White River region. Nevertheless, he loved hunting, fishing, and boating (sometimes even building his own boats). He visited the area often, camping for entire summers at the J.K. Ross homestead, recuperating, and writing.

He served a succession of ministries in Missouri and Kansas. His experiences in Pittsburg, Kansas, resulted in his first novel, *That Printer of Udell's,* published in 1903, a modestly successful book. But his second, *The Shepherd of the Hills,* set in the White River hills, is reported to be the first novel in American history to sell over a million copies. Many of the rest of his novels were set in the Southwest, but his themes remained constant: tales of honor, courage, physical strength, and beauty, and a concern for vanishing peoples and those confronting radical change. His books prominently feature isolated hillfolk of the Ozarks, cowboys of the West, and Native Americans caught on the cusp of progress.

Even today the book that created "The Shepherd of the Hills Country" and formed Branson's identity as a clean, family vacation spot, sells well, and millions of tourists have attended the outdoor drama based on it.

Above left. *Wright, the tall, well-dressed man in the center, on the set of one of his movies. He was an astute businessman involved in the financing and production, as well as the scripting, of many of the pictures made of his novels.*

Above right. *Such was Harold Bell Wright's popular reputation in the teens and twenties that posters for movies made from his books featured his name and likeness rather than the stars.*

THE SHEPHERD OF THE HILLS HOMESTEAD AND OUTDOOR THEATRE

As early as 1909, tourists arriving by train sought out the cabins described in *The Shepherd of the Hills*. The Ross cabin was empty, because the family had moved to Garber to open a store near the railroad. Tourists took souvenirs and carved their names on the walls. The site continued to deteriorate until Miss Elizabeth ("Lizzie") McDaniel, daughter of a wealthy Springfield banker, bought the Ross homestead in 1926. She spent the rest of her life restoring it, collecting memorabilia of the family, and periodically presenting outdoor dramas based on the novel.

Miss Lizzie, as she was affectionately known, left the property to the Branson Civic League, which fulfilled her wish to see that her life's work would be carried on by leasing, in 1946, and later selling the property to Dr. Bruce Trimble and his wife, Mary. The Trimbles, a highly educated, artistic couple, continued the work of preserving and restoring the Homestead. After Dr. Trimble's death in 1957, their son Mark joined his mother in this endeavor. In 1960, they opened "The Old Mill Theatre," where *The Shepherd of the Hills* drama has been performed regularly ever since.

In 1985 Mark Trimble sold the Homestead and Outdoor Theatre to its present owners, Gary and Pat Snadon. Gary Snadon, a former high school football coach in Branson, once played Wash Gibbs, head of the Baldknobbers, in the play.

Here, only a few miles west of the mostly cheerful congestion of 76 Country Boulevard, the pace is calmer, the air is quieter, and it is possible to imagine the life and times of the author and characters of that once wildly popular melodrama. The cabin built by John Ross in 1884 stands on the same spot. (The Rosses, John and Anna, provided the real-life patterns for the central characters, Old Matt and Aunt Mollie, which Wright created.) Some of the Rosses' personal possessions, retrieved by Elizabeth McDaniel in the 1920s, furnish and decorate the cabin.

Tickets to the daytime Homestead include a Jeep-drawn tour of the grounds, horseback trail rides, and a wagon ride up to Inspiration Tower, as well as a trip to the top of the Tower itself for an even grander view.

Old Matt's Cabin, then and now. The cabin was built by John Keever Ross in 1884. He and his wife, Anna, provided the models for Old Matt and Aunt Mollie in Wright's novel. The early photo postcard shows the cabin before the addition of the fireplace and improvements to the front porch rendered it even more picturesque. Today's tourists have their picture taken at this most photographed site in the "Shepherd of the Hills Country."

Every summer evening at 8:30, the play, *The Shepherd of the Hills,* is presented on the 80-yard-long stage, under the stars, to the strong accompaniment of local tree frogs, cicadas, and occasional heat lightning. When a novel is truncated into a play it often requires many regroupings of locations and events to get the basic story told; the same is true of this hearty old morality tale. Still, this is a tale with action and passion and livestock . . . 80 actors (some of whom also hawk souvenir programs and teasingly harass the audience before the performance), 60 head of livestock (you know, sheep, horses, mules), more or less, and special effects. There are guns a-blazin' (which usually start the babies in the audience crying), a knife fight, racing horse teams, a cabin torched by vigilantes (the acrid smell of kerosene and smoke drifts across the theater), and even ghosts. Still, the bad guys are really bad, the good girl is above reproach, and good will and virtue finally triumph.

The backdrop for the play is the reconstructed sawmill owned by Old Matt (John Ross).

"Baldknobbers" were a real life vigilante organization that terrorized the area in the 1880s. Their night-riding activities only stopped after three were publicly hanged on the courthouse square in Ozark, Missouri.

Statue of Old Matt on Inspiration Point. A sculpture garden below the Tower contains statues of the principal characters in the play. The art contest held in the early 1950s to select the design of the first figure, The Shepherd, was judged by Thomas Hart Benton. Today, in the far distance, one can glimpse the waters of Table Rock Lake.

The coming of the railroad greatly accelerated commercial timbering in the upper White River. Previously, logs were rafted on the White to railheads downstream. The fears that Wright voiced through the old shepherd concerning the coming of the railroad were prophetic. The railroad, however, also brought a renewable cash crop: tourism.

The stranger seated himself upon the rude steps. Below and far away he saw the low hills, rolling ridge on ridge like the waves of a great sea, until in the blue distance they were so lost in the sky that he could not say which was mountain and which was cloud. His poet heart was stirred at the sight of the vast reaches of the forest all shifting light and shadows; the cool depths of the nearby woods with the sunlight filtering through the leafy arches in streaks and patches of gold on green; and the wide, wide sky with fleets of cloud ships sailing to unseen ports below the hills.
— *Harold Bell Wright*, THE SHEPHERD OF THE HILLS

Visitors to the homestead today can stand on the spot where Harold Bell Wright pitched his tent those several summers to write *The Shepherd of the Hills*. Looking toward Branson across 76 Country Boulevard and its traffic of motorhomes, tour buses, cars, and vans, a visitor can still see those same hills roll off into the sky. Only a distant glimpse of the waters of Table Rock Lake would differ from the view Wright himself had.

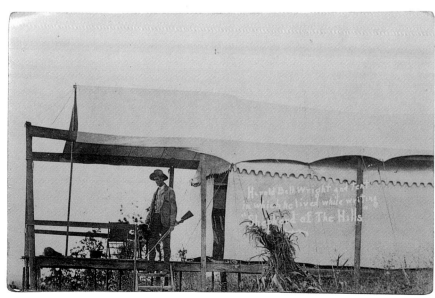

View from the observation deck of Inspiration Tower.
The 230-foot tower was built on Inspiration Point, where
Harold Bell Wright lived in his tent while writing his famous novel.

THE HILLBILLY IMAGE

The railroad brought strangers into hill country, not all of them by any means as sympathetic as Harold Bell Wright. The hillpeople were suspicious of the changes introduced by the "furners." Conversely, the visitors often saw native Ozarkers as, in Vance Randolph's phrase, "the most deliberately unprogressive people in the United States." It was during this era that American popular culture invented the stereotypical "hillbilly."

Mountainous regions are generally poor locations for growing cities or cash crops, traditional sources of wealth. Extracting minerals and cutting timber may create brief booms, but even then the money usually flows out of the region. Rugged terrain inhibits travel. Isolation from urban ways may promote the idea that those who live in the hills are backward, even ignorant. When prosperity seems synonymous with progress, jokes about naive dwellers in the sticks must be expected and hillfolk must endure them. When up-to-date industrial/urban civilization is in a period of decline, however, being a rather conservative, down-home kind of rustic doesn't seem like such a bad deal. It may, in fact, be an attractive alternative.

American slang for rural people contains many negative characterizations: chaw bacon, hayseed, rube, sodbuster, yokel, and, of course, the less pejorative "hillbilly." The word first showed up in print on the 23rd of April, 1900, in a *New York Journal* article defining hillbilly as a "free and untrammelled white citizen of Alabama who lives in the hills, has no means to speak of, dresses as he can, talks as he pleases, drinks whiskey when he gets it, and fires his revolver as the fancy takes him." This is, of course, the standard caricature of Southern hillfolk, a vaudeville, movie, and comic strip staple. Like all cliches, it contains some elements of truth along with the exaggeration. Unlike many other American stereotypes, the hillbilly is rarely so negatively depicted as to disregard his native wit and musical talent. Hollywood's "hick flicks" of the 1930s through the '50s of Ma and Pa Kettle or The Weaver Brothers and Elvira (who, by the way, owned a vacation cabin on Lake Taneycomo) were corny, but all the characters were depicted as admirable folks and, above all, *entertaining*. The conflict between devious Hollywood ways and honest hillbilly values also provided the theme of the successful 1960s television series, *The Beverly Hillbillies*.

Though short on education, comic book hillbillies like Li'l Abner were nevertheless sincere, honorable, and completely unconcerned by their lack of money or social standing. Pop culture hillbillies may be cartoonish, but many exhibit the redeeming values of loyalty to family and friends, unpretentiousness, and a humorous realism concerning the prospect and benefits of wealth. Many Americans today may feel such naiveté is not so dumb after all. Hillbilly ways are, as Vance Randolph pointed out, close to what the United States was originally all about, long ago before the mass market mega-state replaced our individualistic, agrarian democracy.

As the audience gathers at The Shepherd of the Hills Outdoor Theatre, a hillbilly comedian entertains with jokes "that are nobody knows how old," but are nevertheless still funny.

Pop culture icons spin in the breeze along a Branson area highway.

Hillbilly souvenirs from the 1960s display that era's taste for satiric stereotypes.

The hillbilly image is used to advertise the downhome and delicious country fare offered by the Hillbilly Inn.

*Views of Powersite Dam and
Lake Taneycomo, then and now.*

Powersite Dam, Lake Taneycomo
In the Beautiful Ozarks

TANEYCOMO TO TABLE ROCK: THE CURTAIN SLOWLY RISES

It was raining hard when the gates of Powersite Dam were closed for the first time on the free-flowing White River, May 9, 1913. Lake Taneycomo filled in less than two days. Engineers had thought it would take two months. In the 46 years between Lake Taneycomo's creation by a private hydroelectric company and the completion of Table Rock Dam by the U.S. Army Corps of Engineers in 1959, America would fight two world wars, suffer a Great Depression, nearly double its population, and become a global superpower. The farms and small towns carved from the wilderness would themselves diminish drastically. Cities and their suburbs would prosper and grow. Machinery would do the labor once done by men, horses, and mules.

In the White River hills of Harold Bell Wright's novel and along the placid shores of Lake Taneycomo, the Arcadian spirit prevailed. These years were by no means idyllic for everyone (the 1930s were trying times for all Americans), but the lifestyle of both the native Ozarker, conservative by nature, and most of the outsiders who came to live or visit for a spell stood in sharp contrast to the mainstream, go-get-'em, commercial spirit of that era. On the shores of the new lake small hotels and cabins were constructed of native materials. Summer camps thrived. The tourist could detrain at Branson or Hollister and not only float, fish, and explore the White River and Shepherd of the Hills country, but also take a short passenger cruise to the new resort village of Rockaway Beach.

An Arts and Crafts rusticity settled in and stayed longer here than most places in America. The new blue skies of linen postcards capture the carefree, unnumbered days of a summer's stay. Arcadian souls who made Branson and the surrounding hills their home included some prominent artists and writers such as Rose O'Neill, Vance Randolph, and John G. Neihardt. Many other kindred spirits also loved the natural beauty of the Ozarks and revered the folkways of the settlers.

Today's trout fisherman may forget that Lake Taneycomo was once a warm-water lake teeming with bass, crappie, and catfish.

TANEYCOMO HOTEL, TANEYCOMO, MO.   1A2716

Artful rusticity became the dominant style of the day on Lake Taneycomo. A clean, innocent, outdoors life was pursued with considerable success in the White River hills and on the shores of the new lake.

A GOOD DAYS CATCH AT LAKE TANEYCOMO, MO.   4469-29

The OZARKS

The Land of a Million Smiles

BATHING IN LAKE TANEYCOMO, Y.M.C.A. HOLLISTER, MO.

IN THE OZARKS, "THE LAND OF A MILLION SMILES"

COON CREEK BRIDGE, BRANSON-HOLLISTER, MO. HIGHWAY

THE LOG CABIN HOTEL HOLLISTER MO.

Cooperative marketing of the Branson region is a widely recognized component of its current success as one of America's leading family vacation destinations. That idea is not new. Before 1920 towns and vacation attractions throughout southwest Missouri and northwest Arkansas pooled their advertising budgets to publish and distribute brochures touting the many outdoor vacation opportunities of the Ozarks. Organized in 1919, the Ozark Playgrounds Association publicized "the true Ozarkian spirit of hospitality and fair dealing." The copywriters of these promotional pieces for O.P.A. seem to have risen to the challenge of Harold Bell Wright's laudatory descriptive prose in praising the beauty of the area:

A vacationist will find the moonlight streaking its broad golden path across the placid mirror surface of a lake, or the drifting, haunting melodies of the dance orchestra especially appealing. Description might be carried on endlessly, pictures painted as these are, with impartial truthfulness. Probably there still would be omitted the one impression which differs with each – the inherent feeling of having gained and stored in the inner consciousness an individual message which the Ozarks can reveal only to those who come with open heart to gather the recreation, happiness and health the "Land of a Million Smiles" has to offer.

— *The Ozarks.* The Ozark Playgrounds Association, 1929.

THE OZARK SMILE GIRL

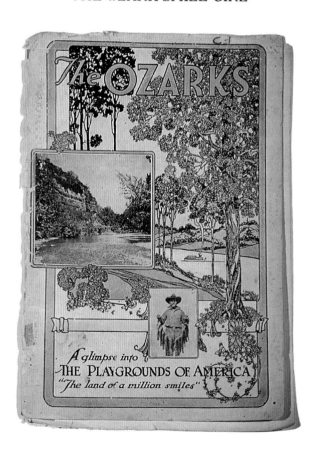

Downtown Branson during
Ozark Mountain Christmas.

In contrast to stores in many
modest-sized towns, many
home-owned and -operated
businesses are thriving in
downtown Branson.

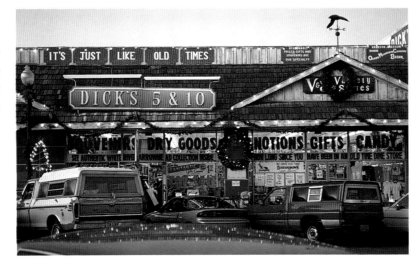

THE COMMERCIAL HOTEL   BRANSON MO.

Branson

Two decades before the railroad brought the town to life a country store stood where Roark Creek flowed into the White River. Reuben Branson, frontier businessman and school teacher, ran the store. When he put in his application for a post office in 1882 he was required to give it a name. The name "Branson" didn't sound too bad to Reuben. He may even have thought it had a distinctive ring. Several years after Branson became a dot on the map, Mr. Branson followed his political star to a job in Forsyth, the county seat. William Hawkins took over his store and post office, but the name "Branson" stayed.

Branson boomed as soon as the route of the White River Line became known. It became a prosperous trade town, shipping railroad ties and later pencils, agricultural products, cotton, cattle, canned tomatoes, and strawberries. Rows of commercial buildings sprang up, burned to the ground, and were quickly rebuilt. The construction of Powersite Dam brought more growth, and by 1912 Branson boasted 1,200 citizens.

Described early on as a town with no saloons or gambling houses, Branson was touted as an ideal environment for healthy outdoor family vacations in a circa-1908 pamphlet put out by the Colony Farm Homes Association. The slightly elevated prose in this booklet, intended to attract both homesteaders and tourists, captures Branson's pastoral aspirations.

The White River country is full of delightful places near the beautiful stream, where, in a cozy cottage or cabin, a family may combine the joys of complete rest and seclusion with life-giving, invigorating sports, and all at a very nominal investment and expense. No place in all the Ozark country excels Branson on the White River, in the natural beauty and attractions of its home sites nor in the advantages and facilities for congenial home-life which it offers with them.

— *Branson, Cottage or Farm Homes.* Issued for Branson Town Company and Branson Commercial Club, Branson, MO, by the Colony Farm Homes Association, St. Louis. Circa 1908.

The old iron bridge that crossed Lake Taneycomo at the end of Main Street was washed away in a flood before Table Rock Dam was built.

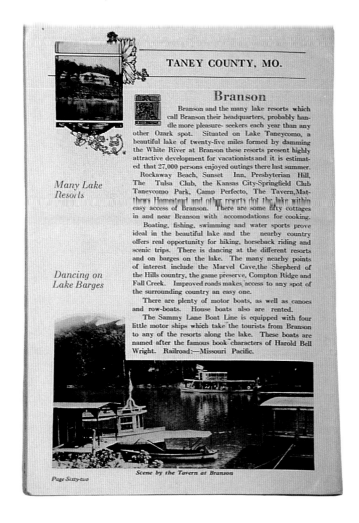

HOLLISTER

Hollister, the village with the Old English-style business district, was a bustling point of departure for many well-heeled, railroad-transported tourists in the early years of tourism. Located south of Branson just across Lake Taneycomo, it had a stylishness rare among small Ozark towns. Much of the town was planned and landscaped according to the vision of a developer and attorney from Springfield named William H. Johnson. He engaged architect Arch Tarbott, also of Springfield, to design the bank building, an inn, and the train depot, all of which still stand.

Like Branson, Hollister has long been the home of numerous festivals and civic organizations, as well as wholesome entertainment for visitors and locals. One of the first things developers did in planning the town was to lay out the Chautauqua Grounds on Presbyterian Hill.

Y. M. C. A. CAMP AT HOLLISTER, LAKE TANEYCOMO, MO.

Much of Hollister is so architecturally distinctive that it is listed on the National Register of Historic Sites.

Before the construction of Table Rock Lake, Hollister was prone to flooding, situated as it is in a narrow valley where Turkey Creek empties into Lake Taneycomo. Here, the rotund guide with the paddle is Jim Owen, famed float trip outfitter.

Ye English Inn still serves the tourist trade, as it did in the early days of Hollister.

Ye English Inn -- HOLLISTER, MO. -- Modern and Fireproof -- On Highway 65

ROCKAWAY BEACH

Another wonderful example of planned rusticity, like the half-timbered Hollister business district, was Rockaway Beach. From the 1920s on, tourists and retirees have appreciated the vision of Willard Merriam and his wife, Anna, who planned and platted this resort community on Lake Taneycomo. Merriam, a Kansas City, Kansas, real estate man, bought 4,600 acres soon after the lake filled. Though the new town was originally called simply Taneycomo, Anna Merriam changed the town's name to Rockaway Beach, after the New York state resort, in the 1920s. The architecture the Merriams promoted was an Ozarkian adaptation of the Adirondacks style: lots of decorative rock work, bent-twig furniture, and varnished cedar and pine interiors. They not only sold lots, but they also built hotels that were operated by family members after his death in 1923 and her death in 1927.

"Pedalos" on Lake Taneycomo, Rockaway Beach, Missouri
In the Beautiful Ozarks

City visitors began many an idyllic vacation in this era by departing from the train in Branson or Hollister for a short cruise down the lake on small passenger and mail boats to Rockaway.

SADIE H.

THE MAIL BOAT
ROCKAWAY BEACH
IN THE OZARKS

REEDS SPRING

Although Reeds Spring's early history was not as touched by tourism as was Branson's or Hollister's, today the town bills itself as "The City of Art." Reeds Spring is home to several galleries and a surprising number and diversity of restaurants, flea markets, and even a club that features alternative music. Pottery and jewelry are made by craftspeople, some of whom have come from as far away as California to live in the Ozarks.

The spring is now covered with a pavilion.

The building of the White River Line turned the area around the spring into a boomtown at the turn of the century. The railroad supplied the needs of laborers who carved a 2,000-foot tunnel through a mountain just east of the town. No easy engineering feat, the building of this tunnel took four years and at its peak employed 250 workers.

Hacking railroad ties from the virgin oak forests was another early industry. Other commercial schemes that have played a part in the history of many Ozark towns are tomato growing and canning and small garment factories.

The present Branson boom is putting a new face on the old commercial buildings in Reeds Spring, which not long ago shared the forlorn look of so many Ozark villages.

Fern falls line the shaded ravines around Reeds Spring. This rustic deer observes tourists from the edge of the parking lot of the Wilderness Clockworks.

The 2,000-foot railroad tunnel near Reeds Spring.

This type of decorative rock work has been called "giraffe stone" by some.
Many such stone cottages are being restored today.

COLLEGE OF THE OZARKS

Known for generations as School of the Ozarks, College of the Ozarks is intimately related to the prosperity of Branson and tourism. Founded in 1906 as a Presbyterian boarding school in Forsyth, its stated purpose was to provide " . . . a Christian education for . . . those found worthy but who are without sufficient means to procure such training." Public schools at that time held classes only three or four months a year, and often instructors had only an elementary education. In seeking to remedy this situation, the Reverend James Forsythe proposed to establish a nine-month school where

students could live (travel was difficult, and many Ozarkers lived in remote areas) and work in exchange for their education. Today it still calls itself "The College that Works," and most of its students (84%) still come from the greater Ozarks region.

After the school's original building burned in 1915 administrators purchased the building and land of The Maine Club on Point Lookout, west of Hollister, where the campus is now located. Although it has evolved from an elementary and high school to a fully accredited four-year college, its mission remains the same: students must demonstrate financial need, academic ability, sound character, and a willingness to work in order to be admitted. The school runs a model farm, a printing plant, a greenhouse that grows the orchids that decorate Shoji Tabuchi's bathrooms, and a mill where meal and flour are ground. It also operates an airport. Students are involved in the maintenance of all these enterprises.

The distinctive buildings were built of native stone from the college's own quarry with student labor. The campus contains The Ralph Foster Museum, "The Smithsonian of the Ozarks," which houses many of the collections of Ralph Foster, the pioneer radio and television producer who produced "Red Foley's Ozark Jubilee" television show in Springfield in the 1950s.

The college's involvement in Branson tourism runs deep: Marvel Cave was donated to the School of the Ozarks by the Lynch sisters, who had leased it to Hugo and Mary Herschend. The College still holds the lease on the cave with the First Presbyterian Church of Branson. Many College of the Ozarks students also staff the rides, ticket booths, and gift shops of Branson area attractions. From its earliest days the College has helped shape and define the image of the Branson area as a hub of vigorous self-improvement and clean, family entertainment.

Facing page.

Left. *Even in the modest early days of School of the Ozarks, now College of the Ozarks, a conspicuous use of native stone was evident in its architecture.*

Right. *The Maine Club building was a well-traveled structure. Built of Maine timber, it was the state of Maine's exhibition building at the St. Louis World's Fair in 1904. The building was purchased by a group of St. Louis businessmen, who had it disassembled and shipped by rail to Branson. It was reassembled on a high ridge above the White River, Point Lookout, and operated as a private club until 1915, when it was purchased by The School of the Ozarks. Dobyns Hall, as it was renamed, burned in 1930.*

Williams Memorial chapel, built in what some call the collegiate Gothic style and dedicated in 1956, stands near the site where The Maine Club once stood.

View from Point Lookout on the campus of College of the Ozarks.

ROSE O'NEILL

Rose O'Neill had already begun her career as one of America's most celebrated illustrators when in 1894 she came to the wilderness cabin her family had homesteaded on Bear Creek, north of Branson. Her art would make her rich, and although she owned estates in Connecticut and Capri, the place she built for her cherished family in the Ozarks was where her heart remained.

It was here, at Bonniebrook, that Rose created her most enduring character, the Kewpie. She said that Kewpies were "benevolent Elves," whose purpose was "to make you laugh, while they do you good." They first appeared in magazines in 1909, and in the more than two decades of their greatest popularity, Rose wrote and illustrated more than 5,000 Kewpie stories. Kewpies adorned comic strips and calendar illustrations. Children asked her for Kewpies they could hold, and she obliged, creating Kewpies in cloth, Kewpies in bisque, and during World War I, Kewpies in celluloid and composition.

Harold Bell Wright, who moved to the Southwest soon after the publication of "The Shepherd of the Hills," found a Kewpie in the desert as he was riding his horse one day. He sent the doll to Rose with a note saying, "Your Kewpies will cover the earth."

Rose and Vance Randolph became friends in the 1930s when he helped her write her autobiography. It has never been published, and apparently only fragments remain.

The "bonnie brook" that Rose O'Neill named her home after, seen in a spring rain. Around the bend and past the overhanging ledge lies the family cemetery, where Rose, her sister, Calista, her mother, Meemie, and brother, Clink, are buried.

Bonniebrook burned in 1947, three years after Rose's death. A new house, built on the original foundation, was reconstructed by the Bonniebrook Historical Society with the aid of the International Rose O'Neill Club. It is open to the public today.

Since 1967, Rose O'Neill fans have come to Branson every April for their annual "Kewpiesta," a weekend of buying, selling, and displaying Kewpie dolls and memorabilia—old, new, and in-between.

The gravel road that today leads from Highway 65 to Bonniebrook. "The next day we went deeper and deeper into the woods. I called it the 'tangle,' and my extravagant heart was tangled in it for good . . . The Forest Enchanted closed us in, and suddenly ahead of us stood Meemie and the other children by the brook."

VANCE RANDOLPH

Vance Randolph's life-long fascination with the music, language, and folkways of the Ozarks resulted in an impressive shelf of books, many popular magazine articles and learned papers, and a colorful but often tough life. Only near the end of his self-appointed career as hillbilly chronicler did Randolph enjoy a modicum of financial security and recognition for his large and delightful body of writing. A flatlander by birth (he was born in Pittsburg, Kansas, in 1892), Vance was of the same fiercely independent turn of mind as the remnants of the old Ozark society he loved and sought to preserve in his work.

Above. *Through most of the 1930s and '40s, Vance Randolph lived in Galena, county seat of Stone County. Galena was also the put-in point of many Ozark float trips that ended in Branson.*

 Right, above. *Randolphs's monumental record of Ozark music and stories went unrecognized by academic folklorists until the very end of his long life. He died in 1981.*

 Right. *Townsend Godsey, himself a chronicler of Ozark folklife, photographed Vance making wire recordings of Ozark folk music for the Library of Congress in the 1930s. (Lyons Memorial Library, College of the Ozarks)*

The James River, which flows past Galena, is still a popular
float stream. The float to Branson, down the James to the
White, originally stretched 125 miles and took five days.
Now floating distance is considerably truncated since the
building of Table Rock Dam filled the lake and backed it
up into the James River arm.

Alice Wright and her great niece, Morgan, on the old Y bridge over the
James River at Galena. Her husband worked as a guide for Jim Owen,
Branson's legendary float outfitter. Mrs. Wright recalled that when the
cost of shipping john boats back to Galena by train rose to $1 per boat,
more than it cost to build them, they were burned as firewood.

Paul Henning, creator/producer of the extremely popular 1960s television series, "The Beverly Hillbillies," wrote in his forward to Owen's book, HILLBILLY HUMOR: "Jim Owen, although he may not know it, has been writing for my program (and probably many others) for years . . . Always on the alert for hillbilly humor, I picked up many of [his] expressions and observations and put them in the mouths of Jed Clampett, Granny, and other characters. It's hard to beat the combination of wit and sagacity in some of those hillbilly expressions . . . In fact, as Jim would say, 'It's harder than sneakin' daylight past a rooster.'"

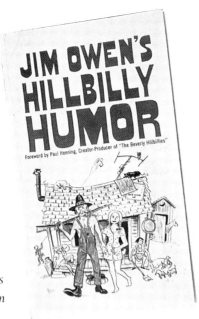

The cast of "The Beverly Hillbillies" met Jim Owen (he's in the center of the back seat) when they filmed several episodes at Silver Dollar City in the early 1960s. Henning took a shine to the area, buying a large park and donating it to the state. The jalopy itself can be seen today at the Ralph Foster Museum at College of the Ozarks. (Lyons Memorial Library, College of the Ozarks)

JIM OWEN

The pristine White River was legendary as a sportsman's paradise. After the railroad was completed float fishing became eminently practical and popular. A fishing party could take a short train ride upstream and float back to Branson, or float downstream from Branson and be picked up. Early on, Branson was the hub of many White River floats. A 1908 booklet describes in detail the types of floats available, costs, and supplies needed.

Jim Owen didn't invent this enterprise, but he became nationally known in the '30s and '40s as *the* float trip outfitter. He believed in the wit and wisdom of native Ozarkers and employed as

Jim's trademark hat.

guides not just the best fishermen, but spinners of the best yarns as well. An Owen float trip often proved to be the experience of a lifetime. Movie stars, prominent politicians, outdoor writers, and generations of fishermen were customers and friends of this Branson businessman.

Owen, a graduate of the University of Missouri, found Branson in the 1920s. In the decades that followed, besides his outfitting business, he built a movie theater and a bowling alley, was elected mayor six times, started a bank, and was a tireless and articulate promoter of the people and the place.

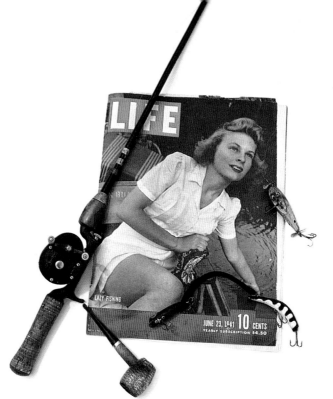

Jim's float fishing business was written up in LIFE, LOOK, SATURDAY EVENING POST, *and repeatedly in hunting and fishing magazines.*

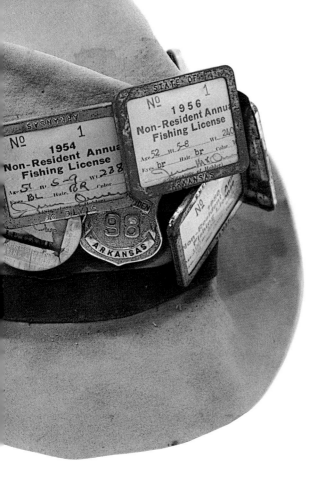

Scale model of the characteristic long, narrow john boats used to float the Ozark streams. At the height of his float fishing business, Jim had forty such boats operating on six rivers and streams. The replica was built by Vi Asselin and Jack Harris of Branson, and the fishermen dolls were created by Mary Crump.

They come to see rugged mountain scenery and quaint log cabins and picturesque rail fences and romantic-looking mountaineers. It is this sort of thing and not mere modern conveniences that pulls the tourist trade. One of Harold Bell Wright's novels got more valuable publicity for the Ozarks than all of the 'booster' associations combined, and the Weaver Brothers have probably brought more tourists into the Ozarks than all of the chambers of commerce in Arkansas.

— Vance Randolph, 1934, defending the commercial adaptation of Ozark folkways.

May Kennedy McCord, "Queen of the Hillbillies," wrote a column entitled "Hillbilly Heartbeats" and had a radio program of the same name in the 1950s and '60s. A Vance Randolph photo. (Lyons Memorial Library, College of the Ozarks)

PEARL SPURLOCK, TYPICAL HILLBILLY AT POWERSITE, MO.

For sixteen years the author of this little volume has operated a taxi for tourists through the country made famous by Harold Bell Wright's story, *The Shepherd of the Hills.* It would be a matter of curious interest to know just how many tires this devoted lady has worn out along the now abandoned goat-trail of a road that climbed the rocky shoulder of Dewey Bald and reached by many rutted crooks and turns the romantic regions that she truly loved and loves.

— John G. Neihardt, epic poet and one-time Branson resident, writing in the foreward to OVER THE OLD OZARK TRAILS *by Pearl Spurlock, 1939.*

Perhaps no other region in the nation fits so snugly in the pocket of the public mind as this Arcadian countryside made famous by Harold Bell Wright nearly half a century ago . . . I first came to the White River country thirty-four years ago (1917) . . . I walked in over the old trail, talked with Uncle Ike and Old Matt, went through Marvel Cave with Wm. Henry Lynch, hiked around the rim of Mutton Hollow, cooked my supper over the coals at Sammy's Lookout, continued on over Dewey Bald, and into Branson and the lake country. We are entering a period of vast recreational development in the Ozarks. National interest in this 'Land of a Million Smiles' is gaining momentum. Branson is the ideal center for this vast activity. The town and its surrounding territory will become more and more a tourist mecca. Lifting my glass of delicious Ozark sassafras tea, I give this toast: 'To Branson, Hollister, and other communities of the famed Shepherd of the Hills/Lake Taneycomo Country, may you continue in the high esteem of the tourist public; may you live long and prosper.'

— Otto Ernest Rayburn, 1951, who through the years published several magazines and books extolling the Arcadian spirit of the Ozarks.

OZARKIAN LORE & LOGIC

The Arcadian years for Branson were between the making of Lake Taneycomo and the construction of Table Rock Reservoir. Tourists arrived by train to begin a carefree outdoors vacation. They could float the clear, fast White River, explore the Shepherd of the Hills country, swim, and play golf or tennis on the shores of Lake Taneycomo. More and more began to arrive by automobile or bus. Perhaps this was not a land that time forgot, but it was a countryside that did its best to preserve a sense of its past. Jazz Age tempos might be briefly heard late at night on a Taneycomo cruise, but the slower heartbeat of the hills still set the pace. Hillbilly ways found many converts, among them movie stars, poets, writers, artists, and independent-minded entrepreneurs who rejected modernism's machine pace. Many came for a visit. Some came to live.

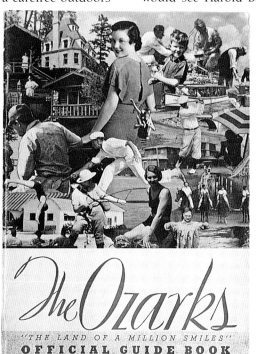

The Branson countryside continues to cast a powerful spell over Americans nostalgic for our rural past. Writers and artists such as Vance Randolph, John G. Neihardt, and Rose O'Neill found surroundings compatible with their romanticism. When vaudeville was terminally wounded by movies, a number of show people opened resorts on Lake Taneycomo. They and many others, native and transplanted, would see Harold Bell Wright's pessimistic vision of the destructive consequences of the coming of the railroad fail to materialize. The wonderous virgin timber did fall to the axe, but the native forests grew back. The song birds, deer, tree toads, and wildflowers survived. The whole landscape and its history were valued by most natives, tourists, and newcomers.

When the curtain rose and multitudes of mobile Americans of the 1950s and 1960s began to discover Branson, they found a set that bore an amazing resemblance to the country Harold Bell Wright had known. It had changed, but it was not as altogether different as Wright had supposed it would be. There still were those who could play a mean fiddle, spin tall tales, or show farmers how to catch smallmouth. Equally important, astute promoters and businessmen recognized the continuing interest Americans had in participating in – not just reading about – our history.

SHOWTIME IN THE OZARKS

High dams on the White River had been envisioned even before the modest structure called Powersite was built early in this century. The engineering know-how and political muscle to build big dams came together in the 1930s, but the Depression and then World War II put many massive federal projects on hold. America rolled into the 1950s with lots of left-over Depression-era mega-plans and a bank account—finally—to afford to build them. The rustic dreamer that was Branson during the 1920s, '30s, and '40s was about to be awakened.

It would not be a traumatic awakening to the Atomic Age. The cultural quakes of the '60s and the after shocks of the '70s were not felt as violently here, either. Branson's historic memories and deep-rooted traditions were challenged again, but not banished.

The dam and the new roads brought hordes of tourists in the late 1950s, '60s, and '70s. They came in two-toned turquoise Detroit chariots, but most came, much in the same way Americans before them had come, looking for some sense of the past they had left behind. But this time there were more, many more. They drove faster and had more money to spend. In Silver Dollar City they found not just a spectacular natural wonder, Marvel Cave, but a virtual movie set of craftspeople, frontier horseplay, and even—just like on TV—gunfights with blanks. The new, bigger lake featured the best bass fishing in the country. Hillbilly music and humor jumped off the front porch and onto the brightly lit stage. It was showtime.

Highway 13 bridge across Table Rock Lake at Kimberling City.
The filling of Table Rock Lake stimulated tourism.

Branson country was, in its way, as novel, different, and rustic to its new visitors in the context of plastic, synthetic, suburban postwar U.S.A. as the wild White River hills had been in Harold Bell Wright's day. It was a refuge, a place to leave the Cold War, rising inflation, and the other ills of modern times behind. The curtain rose, the lights came on, the crowds came, and they loved it all.

The Shepherd of the Hills trout hatchery below Table Rock Dam. Here, some brown but mostly rainbow trout are raised to stock Lake Taneycomo. The Missouri Department of Conservation gives guided tours of the facility.

Table Rock Dam was built by the U.S. Army Corps of Engineers. Construction is well advanced in the 1957 photograph on the facing page. (Lyons Memorial Library, College of the Ozarks)

Greetings From
The Ozarks

New Highway 65 was cut through to Branson in the mid-1960s,
reducing driving time from Springfield by almost half. When
Harold Bell Wright first came to the White River country there
were 8,000 automobiles in the U.S. and 21 million horses.
By 1973, Detroit produced yearly 10 million heavily chromed
passenger cars—some 300- and 400-horsepower—a fair
number of which could be found during the summer months
jamming the parking lots of the Presleys', the Baldknobbers,
The Plummer Family, Foggy River Boys, Silver Dollar City,
and other Branson entertainments.

Ozark Playgrounds

Power boats had a bigger pool to play in
with the completion of Table Rock Lake.

In this new era, the old
attractions continued
to be popular.
These mid-1960s
advertisements promote
the continuing charm
of an old-fashioned
vacation with hillbilly
overtones.

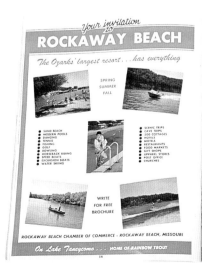

On the road to Branson, 1972.
Cheap gas, big, fast cars,
paid vacations, better roads,
and a clear blue lake contributed
to rapid growth in what was
now called the Tri-Lakes Area.

Red Foley's nationally broadcast "Ozark Jubilee" and Branson's budding local shows caused the writer of an early 1960s "Ozark Guide" to observe: "It is small wonder that the Ozarks have become known, from New York to Hollywood as THE CROSS-ROADS OF COUNTRY MUSIC."

Springfield, a postwar boom town just 40 miles north of Branson, was located on America's Main Street, Route 66 (now I-44). "The Queen City of the Ozarks" is actually situated on gently rolling prairie land with no geographical impediment to commercial development. It has been a transportation hub for over 100 years. Its involvement in Branson's growth has been and continues to be large. In the 1950s Springfield was Nashville's closest rival as a country performance center, all because of a radio show that switched to television: Red Foley's "Ozark Jubilee" Ralph Foster's radio station, KWTO (Keep Watching The Ozarks), which featured many live talent broadcasts, launched the show in July 1954. By early 1955 ABC-TV began weekly coverage. The television show ran for six years and showcased the rising and established stars (Red Foley himself was a member of the Grand Ole Opry) of country music.

Vintage 1950s neon still lights the Jesse James Motel sign on 76 Country Boulevard. In the early 1960s the motel was part of a larger complex including the Jesse James Museum, Outlaw Town, and Confusion Hill. Today neon signage like this is widely recognized as an art form. This superb sign is as legitimate a piece of Americana as a log cabin. Such signs may, ironically, be more endangered than log cabins, however, because they often occupy valuable commercial sites. One can only hope that some examples such as this of Branson's colorful early roadside architecture will survive.

SILVER DOLLAR CITY

Silver Dollar City is a shady park with a sunny disposition. The shade is the legacy of Mary Herschend, mother of the present owners, Jack and Peter Herschend. As she and they worked in the late 1950s to lay out the paths and build the first few buildings of their 1880s craft village at the mouth of Marvel Cave, she insisted that trees not be cut down. Now, as visitors roam the winding streets of the City, even the hottest summer day is made bearable by the rich dappled shadows of the leafy canopy. The sunny disposition is supplied by the 1,100 "citizens" of the City who run the lathes, make the toys, bake the bread, run (or rob) the train, and otherwise entertain.

Silver Dollar City got its name from Don Richardson, head of promotions for Red Foley's "Ozark Jubilee" television show. As Jack Herschend tells it, they were casting about for a name for the old-time town they were building and had about settled

Slip into the past with the tintype photographer's copious collection of old-time costumes.

on "Ozark Mountain Village" when Richardson stepped in. "No," he said. "You don't call it Ozark Mountain Village, because Ozark Mountain Village is a set of adjectives. Branson, Missouri, is an Ozark mountain village. In addition, we have to create a name because we don't have any money for marketing, advertising, publicity. We have to create a name people will remember, have an association with. What we will name it is Silver Dollar City, and the reason we will name it Silver Dollar City is we will give silver dollars in change." And that's precisely what they did for the first two years. The word of mouth advertising this promotion created caused attendance to jump from 50,000 in 1957, when Marvel Cave was the only attraction, to 125,000 in 1960, the year they opened Silver Dollar City with no advertising.

No silver dollars for change any more, but the park has continued to grow. Today, more than one and a half million visitors come to Silver Dollar City every year. Besides the few original old fashioned shops, the City now features working craftsmen and women, as well as rides for the kids, restaurants, and live entertainment. The entertainment ranges from the late Shad Heller's Toby Show to train robbers to conversations with a miner leading his pack mule through town to listening to a hymn sung by the Sheriff in the Wilderness Church. In the evening, after the rides, restaurants, and shops close, the Branson Brothers, a contemporary country group, perform in Echo Hollow Amphitheatre. All these attractions are included in the price of the ticket.

From opening day (the Mabe brothers, now the Bald-knobbers, provided music for the festivities) to the present, Silver Dollar City has been an active park. Besides being a shopping experience, it has a hands-on, how-to, something-going-on-every-minute feel. Whether you happen on a live music show, have a parasol painted, witness a shoot-out, or spin a wishing wheel, you feel a sense of participation, of being part of the show.

A troupe of young cloggers performs at the evening show in Echo Hollow Amphitheatre.

Even into the early 1960s, Marvel Cave was advertised as the main attraction.

Scattered through the park are all kinds of eating establishments from full-service restaurants to cafeterias to quick snacks.

Marvel Cave has been continuously operated as a tourist attraction for almost 100 years. William Henry Lynch, a Canadian government official, purchased the cave in the 1880s (the exact year varies from one account to another) sight unseen. In the early 1890s he opened it to tourists. Lantern-lit tours were often led by Truman Powell, who later became the model for the old shepherd in Wright's *Shepherd of the Hills*. In the 1920s Lynch began building a road around Dewey Bald into Branson to facilitate tourists' travel to the Cave. Many improvements and decades later, this road is now Highway 76. After Lynch died in 1932, his daughters, Genevieve and Miriam, continued to operate the cave until 1949, when they leased it for ninety-nine years to the vacationing Hugo Herschend family of Chicago.

Hugo Herschend's plan was to expand the attractions at Marvel Cave in order to increase tourism. He died in 1954, leaving Mary, the two boys, and a few loyal employees to continue to develop it as a tourist attraction. While he lived, Hugo had spoken of developing an old-time craft village as an attraction, and in the late '50s the idea resurfaced when Charlie Sullivan, an 87-year-old traveling salesman, came to town. He told of being born in a mining town, Marmaros, built at the entrance to the cave. The story goes that he kicked aside a few rocks and leaves, uncovering the foundation of the hotel. How appropriate it seemed, then, to build Hugo's idea on authentic Ozark foundations.

Ozark square dance festivals have been held in the hugo 10-stories-high Cathedral Room in Marvel Cave. 5,000 people can find safety during an atomic attack in this massive natural bomb shelter.

The developers started with a few shops built, as Mary Herschend insisted, with 19th century tools and technology and two restored buildings, the Wilderness Church and the McHaffie Homestead. The idea was that they would give people something to do while they waited for the next tour of the cave. Today, tours of the cave depart hourly (there's plenty of walking, but now a train brings explorers back to the surface), and the park teems with guests from the time it opens to the end of the Branson Brothers' performance.

In the 1950s the Herschends had the Ozarks Jubilee band play for square dances in the Cathedral Room of Marvel Cave.

Marvel Cave's Cathedral Room today as a tour files down the side of the huge talus slope.

Your ticket to Silver Dollar City includes the evening show at Echo Hollow Amphitheatre, where the Branson Brothers entertain under the stars. The nooks and crannies and winding paths of the park have disguised the size of the crowd during the day. Until everyone gathers at the show, few realize how crowded the park has been.

WHITE WATER

The Herschend's theme park interests extend beyond Silver Dollar City. They are in partnership with Dolly Parton in her park, Dollywood, in Pigeon Forge, Tennessee, and they also own several water parks outside of Branson. White Water, their tropical water park on 76 Country Boulevard, features a dozen rides of varying degrees of excitement.

Stub Meadows looks guilty when Droopy Drawers discovers his pet mouse dead in his cup. Mouth to mouse resuscitation doesn't work.

Droopy Drawers (played for 34 years by founding partner Jim Mabe) mimics Joy Bilyeu (a third generation member of the Mabe family) as she sings.

Mike Ito was the first Japanese country fiddle player in Branson. He also does a fancy Swiss yodel. He's been with The Baldknobbers for thirteen years.

THE BALDKNOBBERS

Bill and Jim Mabe have come a long way since they played from a flatbed truck at "Plumb Nelly Days" in Branson, along with brothers Lyle and Bob, in the mid '50s. Soon after that they put on the first bona fide, regularly scheduled music show in Branson, opening in 1959 in the Branson Community Center, downtown in what is now Old Branson, playing two shows a week during the summer. They played for the opening day of Silver Dollar City in 1960 and also for the barn dance scene in "The Shepherd of the Hills." From this latter stint they got the name they have gone by ever since, The Baldknobbers. (The Baldknobbers are the bad guys in the play. In real life they were a post-Civil War vigilante group that roamed the hills of Stone, Taney, and Christian counties until the late 1880s.)

Their audience grew, and with the need for space, The Baldknobbers moved to the Sammy Lane Pavilion on the waterfront, where they played for four years. From there they moved to the skating rink for another four years. Then in 1968 they bought land not far from the Presleys' on Highway 76 and built an 865-seat theater.

"Country Variety" is still their formula for success, and this mixture of songs, new and old, dancing, and lots of costume changes and cornball humor (with plenty of outhouse material, though that may have to change now that the Sears catalog is defunct) still gets a rise out of every house. It's the kind of show where even the most sophisticated will guffaw at well-timed jokes and titter at the behind-the-soloist antics of comic characters Droopy Drawers and Stub Meadows, and get swept up in a stirring patriotic number.

Before the eight o'clock evening show, the arriving audience is treated to a pre-show "warm-up." Joe's Ragtime Parlor takes requests from the audience and encourages their participation, sometimes getting a real trouper or former church choir leader to do the singing.

The Baldknobbers' complex now includes a motel, restaurant, and 1,700-seat theater. The show itself includes three generations of Mabes in a total cast of eighteen.

From a fifty-seat show in the downtown Community Center in 1959 to their 1,700-seat theater with adjoining motel and restaurant on 76 Country Boulevard, The Baldknobbers have come a long way.

The lighting and sound systems have been updated through the years, but their entertainment formula and personal attention to the audience haven't changed.

Sid Sharp (Windy Luttrell), Herkimer (Gary Presley), and Lloyd Presley. Windy Luttrell and Lloyd go 'way back, having picked together on KWTO radio in Springfield in 1948, recorded a couple of songs in Nashville in 1960, and of course, played at the Presleys' since the late '60s. "I would be safe in saying that we've played together longer than anyone else here not in the same family," Windy says.

The hay bales and barn interior set have been left behind but not the Presleys' solid sense of country music or the hilarity of hillbilly humor.

PRESLEYS' JUBILEE

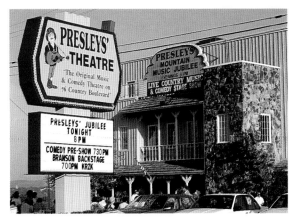

When Lloyd and Bessie Mae Presley and their boys opened their music theater on Missouri Highway 76 on June 30, 1967, they were still working their day jobs. The concrete-floored metal building with stage and folding chairs was the Lone Ranger of theaters several miles from town. As Gary Presley tells it "We put a flat floor in the building because we thought if the show didn't work we might be able to use it for boat storage for people who were having boats over on Table Rock Lake. That's a true story." Today their 2,000-seat, air-conditioned facility is surrounded by other theaters, souvenir shops, restaurants, and motels, and they sing and play to packed houses throughout the season. Soon, their 53-acre campground adjacent to the theater will become the site of a multi-million-dollar hotel-theater-shopping complex, developed with Talentino & Horn of Minnesota's Mall of America.

Some things haven't changed, however, like the Presleys' formula for family entertainment. Lloyd still slaps the upright bass fiddle every night, Gary still plays Herkimer, "the grand clown of country comedy" ("I ain't so dumb—I didn't pay nothin' to get in here"), and Steve pounds the drums. Another generation of Presleys has also joined the show. Gary's and Steve's sons (Scott, Greg, Eric, Nick and John) play and sing with a cast that now numbers more than 20 performers.

The costumes have been updated (gold lamé, sequins, and spangles), and the building has been remodeled and enlarged five times over the years, but the formula remains the same: lots of energetic singing of current hits, country classics, some gospel tunes, and a liberal sprinkling of spoofs, one-liners (Herkimer comes back with a new watch: "Times got so tough, I had to lay off one of my hands"), character parodies, and neighborliness (the audience is invited to "Come on down and say hi to us," during intermission).

Third generation Presleys, Greg (on harmonica) and Scott. Greg credits the Presleys' success to "twenty-five years of families coming back."

CAMPBELL'S OZARK COUNTRY JUBILEE

The name sounds familiar because it actually came from Red Foley's 1950s television program. Warren Stokes, who had a theater in Springfield in the early 1970s, bought the name from Ralph Foster's organization. He moved his show to Branson in 1980 after buying the Ozark Hayride building from Elmer Dryer. In 1985, Maggie Sue and Clifford Campbell took over the Jubilee and added their name to the title.

The Jubilee is a busy place, offering four shows a day: shows by the Jubilee cast as well as touring national acts. Some of their success in competing with the nationally known entertainers who've recently come to town can be attributed to their fans. While all the local shows have a history of touring during the winter months through small towns in the Midwest and South, the Jubilee has a particularly avid group of fans in Maurice, Iowa. Every April the cast of the Jubilee spends a week in Maurice (pop. 283), and the town booster club brings in bus tours to hear them from as far away as South Dakota. The red carpet rolls out in front of the First Reformed Church, flags decorate the town, and the Mayor and Little Miss Maurice greet their visitors. It's like old home week for the cast and the town. "When the Jubilee comes each April," says Mayor VanDerWeide, "it's like family coming home."

Campbell's Ozark Country Jubilee presents one of the more exuberant facades to 76 Country Boulevard.

The Brown Sisters, Okie and Dava,
from Oklahoma, are backup and
featured singers at the Jubilee.

Eddie Rabbit ("The Wanderer") wandered
into Campbell's with his Hare Trigger Band
and played 70-plus dates at the Jubilee
through the 1993 season. His hit singles
"Drivin' My Life Away," "I Love a Rainy
Night," and "Step by Step," bring
appreciative hoots and applause from the
audience. Before he became a headliner, this
Brooklyn-born son of Irish immigrants had
written "Kentucky Rain" for Elvis and
"Pure Love" for Ronnie Milsap.

FOGGY RIVER BOYS & BOB-O-LINKS

The Foggy River Boys opened the third theater on 76 Country Boulevard in 1974. They had performed their four-part harmony in gospel and country music in Kimberling City for three years before that (price of admission in 1972: $2 adults, 50¢ children). The original cast retired in 1992, and The New Foggy River Boys opened in 1993 in the same distinctive theater.

The fifth theater to open on what was then called "the strip" was built by Bob Mabe, one of the original Baldknobbers, who branched out on his own. He opened Bob-o-Links Country Hoe-Down in April 1977 with Ronnie Milsap as guest star. Bob Mabe was a pioneer in bringing nationally known acts to Branson. The roster of those who have played his theater reads like a Who's Who of country music. He also designed the eighteen-foot-high fiddlin' hillbilly that stood in front of the theater for years. After Bob retired in 1986, the theater became home to The Texans, and the hillbilly turned into a long, tall Texan. In 1992 the building briefly housed the Celebration Theatre, a gospel show, but in 1993 the Osmond Family Theater occupied the remodeled premises.

TENT SHOW TIME

Once upon a time, most Americans lived in the country or in small towns that provided the material needs of the farmer and his family. Before radio or television, before movies, books, magazines, and newspapers served to inform and educate. The need for entertainment, live and lively, however, was so great in the sticks that everyone for miles around would show up for such dubious spectacles as a single very old elephant or a public hanging. Anything remotely out of the ordinary would draw a crowd. Traveling shows of various kinds played to sell-out crowds in the rural U.S. in the late 1800s and early 1900s before the advent of modern media. Whether moralistic and serious like the Chautauqua, exotic like the circus, thrilling like carnival rides, or musically compelling like the hillbilly and minstrel music of the medicine shows, these roving entertainments provided rich experiences for rural and small town audiences.

To be sure, most burgs had brass bands to back up the oratory of patriotic holidays. Most households had parlor organs or pianos, and unmarried females of varying ages and musical abilities would, with little or no persuasion, render popular sheet-music songs. These poles of the predictable and the private, however, did not discharge the energy that rural American life generated. No matter what crises and misfortunes later befell rural and small-town America, the 19th century was a wonderful and optimistic time to be alive. Into this rural entertainment vacuum came the summer tent show.

These rural and small-town tent shows were, of course, rendered obsolete by movies, radio, and television. A nostalgia for live entertainment of this type lingered, however, and in the 1960s Branson began to supply shows akin to the earlier tent shows. Taken as a totality, Branson shows are amazingly similar in format to these long-gone entertainments of music and comedy for the entire family. Ropes, poles, and canvas have been replaced by steel and concrete, finished out with the most up-to-date composites and synthetics, the whole announced in neon. The crowd comes to the theater, instead of the theater coming to town. They arrive, some from long distances, by automobile and bus to the Branson theaters expecting and receiving "a decent alternative to epics, orgies, sex, and horror," as an astute observer once described the virtues of Southern and Midwestern tent shows.

Tom and Jaynee Vandenberg, vaudevillians at Mutton Hollow.

85

COUNTRY THEMES

The federally financed roads and reservoirs brought hordes of mostly rural, small-town, and working-class Americans to Branson and The Shepherd of the Hills Country in the 1960s and '70s. There they found entertainments that reflected their values: the importance of family, traditional religion, patriotism, individuality, friendliness, and a healthy respect for hands-on skills such as crafts or playing a stringed instrument. Branson sported its pioneering music and comedy shows, Silver Dollar City, The Shepherd of the Hills, and expanded opportunities for vigorous outdoor recreation.

During this same time commercial network television programmers concluded that entertainment with a country flavor didn't attract the more "sophisticated" urban and suburban audience that they increasingly targeted. "Gunsmoke," "HeeHaw," "The Beverly Hillbillies," "Lawrence Welk," "Green Acres," "Petticoat Junction," and "Mayberry, R.F.D." were all cancelled in the early 1970s, despite their popularity, because their audience was considered too old and too rural. Every one of these shows has gone on to huge success in syndication and more recently on videotape. Many can still be seen daily on cable. Most of the urban/suburban programs that replaced these shows are now little more than obscure questions on quiz shows.

Today Roy Clark ("HeeHaw") has his "Celebrity Theatre," and Jim Nabors (from "The Andy Griffith Show," which sired "Mayberry, R.F.D.") is a frequent guest artist. Larry Welk, Lawrence's son, is building "The Champagne Theater." Paul Henning, creator of "The Beverly Hillbillies," "Petticoat Junction," and other country comedies, was himself a Branson fan. Several episodes of "The Beverly Hillbillies" were filmed at Silver Dollar City. He donated the Ruth and Paul Henning Park around Dewey Bald to the State and the Hillbillies' jalopy to the Ralph Foster Museum.

Country themes thrived in Branson at the very time when they were considered unprofitable, and therefore unfashionable, in the mass media. The loyal audience that Madison Avenue dismissed came back year after year. It was truly "country when country (and Western and hillbilly) wasn't cool."

1972. Branson was "country when country wasn't cool."

Sign for Silver Mine Theater

Neon signs, early television, and jukeboxes are the
nostalgic symbols for Baby Boomers. The artful use
of neon in Branson is neither glarish nor garish.
Instead, it is used to accent the fanciful architecture
of entertainment.

STARS, CARS, AND ELECTRIC GUITARS

Country music is, was, and always will be largely created by and appreciated by rural people. From time to time, however, city folk prick up their ears, kick up their heels, and discover some of its many charms. American consumer society runs on fads, and usually after a time of I-can't-get-enough-of-that (be it Hawaiian music, blues, jazz, rock, rap, pop, do-wop, or country) they dance on. A flick of the wrist, a twist of the dial, and another sound is found.

The huge national acceptance of country today began building in the late 1970s and early '80s. The political success of the Reagan-Bush years was reflected in the growth of Branson in the '80s as a venue of country music. Yet country music is not inherently politically partisan. There are probably as many Democrats playing fiddle as there are Republicans. But it is God-fearing, patriotic, and individualistic. And it was goin' strong before we were even a country. It is traditional, conservative, and entrepreneurial. This appealed to the G.I. generation, which was feeling increasingly alienated from the sex and violence in movies, television, records – indeed, from all media. Branson is a refutation of the frequent Hollywood disclaimer, when asked about exploding cars, steamy sex scenes, guns, and mayhem in general: "We're only giving them what they want." Truth is, sex, violence, and special effects are cheaper and easier to produce than stories about real people that involve real talent on all levels. If Branson is about anything, it is about individual choice, seeking out entertainment that corporate culture has branded unpopular, unsophisticated, unnecessary.

Branson is the result of low overhead, loyal audiences, a relentless desire to perform, old-fashioned Mom-and-Pop capitalism, and a conspicuous absence of middle-men (i.e., the small army of agents, managers, bodyguards, lawyers, and critics that gets between the talent and their fans). The modern machinery that creates product – movies, records, television programming – was never installed in Branson. Branson was built on live performance, and it often has the informality of a long-ago pie supper. Today, the performers may still stop by your tour bus after the show for a snapshot and an autograph.

Just guess what kind of people play country music. The players share the values of their audience. It's not an act. Branson's laid-back, laissez faire approach to music, comedy, and business caught the attention of other country performers in the '80s. There was that – and then there was that matter of all those cars, bumper to bumper on 76 Country Boulevard: all those cars (and trucks and RVs) with all those passengers, buying tickets, coffee mugs, T-shirts, tapes, and even Frisbees emblazoned with the star's logo. The stars began to find the cars and a home base and in the 1980s they plugged their electric guitars into Branson's dynamic current.

Branson in the '80s began to reflect a mixture of generational nostalgia. Memories of log cabins faded. Early cars and tin advertising signs became fond remembrances for G.I. generation tourists. In the early years, Branson had rusticity and running water. Today, the car looks old-time, but everything about it is up to date: it's a 1980s replica of a Model A Roadster with automatic transmission.

During the '80s an increasing number of businesses offered entertainment, souvenirs, lodging, and food to increasing lines of traffic on 76 Country Boulevard. This bumper-to-bumper traffic may have been a source of humor, but it also alerted the world at large that something important was going down in a little Ozark town off the beaten track. Jokes in the shows about the traffic have a touch of amazement in their tone — a sort of "where'd-all-those-people-come-from, ain't-we-glad-they're-here" combination of puzzlement and pride. And the people in the traffic have a cheerful sense of their own stately promenade: a country style automotive stroll on Branson's version of the Boardwalk or the Avenue: the slow, polite progress down 76 Country Boulevard, where cars turning left are let through, horns don't honk, and passengers converse with pedestrians.

ROY CLARK

Roy Clark took a shine to Branson early in the '80s. He likes golf and fishing. He likes picking and singing for live audiences. And he has grown accustomed to running his own life the Roy Clark way. Branson seemed like the place to do it all.

Roy earned his star in Branson's Hall of Fame (if one is ever built) when he became the first nationally known country musician to establish a permanent theater in Branson. In 1983 he opened his Roy Clark Celebrity Theatre on 76 Country Boulevard. The "Celebrity" in its title was not just for Roy. Since the theater opened a whole constellation of country music stars has gathered along this ridge-top road to play his stage. For a number of them, this introduction to Branson's music scene served as a port of entry, and they now host their own shows on or near 76 Country Boulevard. Familiar personal-ities like Mel Tillis, Ray Stevens, Mickey Gilley, Jim Stafford, and Boxcar Willie played and stayed. Others like Ray Price, Johnny Paycheck, Jim Nabors, Tammy Wynette, Tanya Tucker, and the late Roger Miller, to name only a few, have come and gone and often returned.

Some musicians play fast, and the crowd loves it. Often, however, the tunes that are dancing through their ears at 115 m.p.h. are trick tunes that don't require as much musicianship as the audience supposes. Every so often there comes along a Roy Clark who can play fast *and* good, or slow and good. With a wild sense of humor and free flowing energy, he not only plays fast, but also drag races for fun and charity, flies his own Steerman stunt plane, and tells jokes – funny ones – at a rapid-fire rate that hits the mark. Not surprisingly, Roy

put together a band of virtuoso players and merry musical pranksters.

Roy has an amazing reper-toire – and can play it all at any tempo, in any style. His prodi-gious creativity has taken such diverse forms as co-hosting "HeeHaw," perhaps the most suc-cessful television show in syndi-cation, and having an album rated five-star by the jazz mag-azine *Downbeat*.

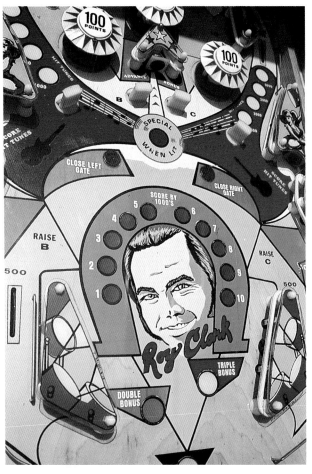

The ultimate Roy Clark collectible: "Super Picker Roy Clark" pinball machine. Knowing Roy's dexterity, it's likely he can beat anyone on his own game.

The parade of stars who come through Roy Clark's Celebrity Theatre keeps the people who keep the marquee up to date busy. Roy's theater has been the port of entry into Branson for a number of nationally known stars who now have their own theaters.

If by a person's twelfth birthday he's won the state fiddling or picking contest, he's ready to audition for Roy's band. Such talent is rare, and many members of his all-virtuoso band have been with Roy for years.

This striking sign announced Mickey Gilley's theater before the fire.
Untouched by disaster, the sign may soon light your way to the new Gilley's.

Mickey plays a boogie-bluesy piano style "created by my first cousin,
Jerry Lee Lewis — just ask him."

MICKEY GILLEY

Mickey Gilley pours a 90-proof shot of Southern soul into Branson's music mix. Born in Mississippi and raised in Ferriday, Louisiana (learning church music there with first cousin Jerry Lee Lewis and second cousin Jimmy Swaggart), Mickey brings the heat of the night to his Branson stage. Seated at the grand piano, Gilley's left hand pounds out a blues that would rock New Orleans. Then the voice with seventeen number one singles moves west and becomes the heart of Texas. As if this music alone wasn't worth the price of a ticket, Mickey Gilley tells his compelling story as architect of the *Urban Cowboy* rage in the late 1970s.

At its peak, Gilley's, in Pasadena, Texas, could quench the thirst of 4,500 cowboys and cowgirls (by day most were oil workers and waitresses). Mickey didn't see eye to eye with his business partner, however, and the famous mechanical "El Toro" threw its last rider in the late 1980s. Gilley showed up in Branson, and after a few gigs at Roy Clark's, bought the Country Music World Theater. In a season, he began to find deep satisfaction in developing into a consummate live entertainer. His voice is clear and strong today, and the rewards of dealing with a sober audience pleased the former impressario of the most renowned honky tonk of all time. It looked like Mickey had a warehouse full of roses, when early in the 1993 season double tragedies struck. A neon transformer in his theater started an electrical fire that destroyed the lobby and damaged the rest of the theater so badly it had to be torn down. ("You didn't know we had the hottest show in town," he teases an audience.) Then on June 5th his old friend, the great Conway Twitty, who had alternated dates with Mickey, died of an abdominal aneurysm.

Boxcar Willie generously offered Mickey a stage across the street, and his show went on. Mickey himself drove a bulldozer (he was in construction before music) to clean up the wreckage. He is a man of many talents, a man capable of periodic reinvention. Undoubtedly, Mickey Gilley's new Branson theater will be as successful as his spellbinding music.

Mickey Gilley commands the Urban Cowboy Band, "the only Grammy award-winning band in town."

MOE BANDY'S AMERICANA THEATRE

Moe Bandy is a charter member of Branson's Texas Connection. Like his friends Boxcar Willie and Mickey Gilley, he has deep roots in hard-living, sweet-singing, pure country. It is a music whose diverse origins can be found in rural church music; honky tonks inhabited by hard hats, cowboys, and pretty girls; and black blues, occasionally sauced by a Mexican musical influence. If it's anything, it's vigorous, and if it'll live in Texas, you can transplant it anywhere.

Moe went from the job security of rodeo riding to a life of even greater security playing honky tonks. Gifted with an extraordinarily clear singing voice, he has a laconic, cowboy-type sense of humor. Country music is a shared experience that includes a sense of personal identification with the song and the singer. Moe knows that. Expanding his repertoire to include contemporary hits without sacrificing his extreme honesty, he projects this sincerity in his conversational style of singing. Viewed by scholars of country music as an important link between the raw honesty of 1940s and '50s honky tonk and the current wave of new traditionalists, Moe preserves this place in his shows at the Americana Theatre.

He opened his show in 1991 after buying the theater from the Plummer Family, one of the pioneer shows on 76 Country Boulevard (they were the fourth show on the strip, opening in 1973).

Patriotism is the theme of Moe Bandy's Americana Theatre. His red, white, and blue electric light bunting facade sparkles just east of Presleys' Mountain Music Jubilee.

Terri Williams does impersonations of six different country singers, complete with lightning-fast costume changes, during Moe's show. Moe eggs her on, faster and faster, while he does his own versions of Elvis, George Jones, and others.

During each show Moe comes out into the audience to sing and greet his guests. His is a relaxed, easy-going show, where visitors always feel welcome.

BOXCAR WILLIE

Trains, planes, and guitars are only a few of the toys Boxcar Willie likes to play with. Next to his music hall is a museum full of rare country music memorabilia, as well as the very cockpit of a KC-97 flying tanker where Master Sergeant Marty Martin of the Air National Guard entertained the crew with cowboy songs and hillbilly humor. ("Were you a pilot or a flight engineer?" a man calls from the audience. "Neither. My parents were married," Boxcar counters.) Born Lecil Travis Martin in Texas, he acquired a love of country music and railroads from his father, a track foreman on the KATY and fiddle player.

Gifted with one of the purest country voices since his idol, Jimmie Rodgers, Marty Martin headed for Nashville after 22 years in the service. Nashville didn't take much notice at first. He was "discovered" at an English music festival by Wesley Rose of Acuff-Rose Publishing and soon became a regular on the Grand Ole Opry.

After several guest appearances in the Branson area, he bought the empty Wilkinson Brothers theater down the road from Roy Clark's Celebrity Theatre and opened his show in 1987.

A trainman's holiday: Boxcar Willie hops a streamlined 1940s dome car on the Branson Scenic Railway's initial run.

Backing up Boxcar's extraordinarily strong ▶
voice is a band that plays pure country,
The Texas Trainmen. Each of his loose, relaxed
shows is videotaped, with generous camera
sweeps of the audience, and you can order your
own copy of the very show you saw.
Maybe the kids back home will be able
to see Mom and Dad, Row 23, center.

Ventriloquist Patty Davidson rips through her ▶
breakneck, up-dated vaudeville/baseball
routine with friends Dan the Man and Lucy.

A visitor can hardly miss Boxcar's signage:
blue neon smoke rolls from the engines as the
red neon wheels turn. On a brightly lit
showbiz strip, this theater still stands out.

Chisai (pronounced Chee-sigh) Childs, sometimes called the "Belle of Branson," who has been associated with the Branson show scene for many years, is considered one of the founders of the fast-paced, Branson-brand variety show with a country flavor.

COMMUNITY SPIRIT

Branson has always been a get-along town, with a lot of diverse civic organizations and charities. A long tradition exists in the entertainment world of lending one's talent to worthy causes, and Branson stars whole-heartedly embrace that tradition. All the stars who came to Branson in the '80s and '90s participate in fund-raising for local causes, as well as their favorite national charities. They have, in turn, enlisted the casts of Branson's pioneering shows to appear on telethons such as the Jerry Lewis Muscular Dystrophy Association telethon, segments of which were broadcast from the Mel Tillis Theater. During the great summer floods of 1993, Wayne Newton sponsored a nationally televised all-star fund raiser for flood relief that was broadcast from his theater. "Hey, kids! We can help! Let's put on a show!" was the order of the day, as the show was produced in only one week.

National events and local causes: both get the attention and support of Branson personalities and entertainers as these portraits shot at The Ozarks Literacy Council's annual banquet attest. Many stars who couldn't come (they do two shows a day, after all) sent representatives with checks.

Two of Branson's better known Texas transplants give literacy thumbs up: Moe Bandy and Boxcar Willie.

Ron and Pam Blackwood. Ron is a member of The Blackwood Quartet.

Denzel Koontz, member of the original Foggy River Boys. Even after they retire, many performers stay in the Branson area and continue to pitch in.

Clockwise from left.

David Slater, a winner of "Star Search," sings at the Mel Tillis Theater.

Jennifer Wilson of "Jennifer in the Morning."

The Norris Twins, Becky and Lindy, well-known Branson entertainers.

Philip Wellford, juggler and comedian at Andy Williams' Moon River Theatre.

Janet Dailey, best-selling romance novelist and long-time Branson resident. She and her husband, Bill Dailey, have been shapers of the Branson dream.

Christina Tabuchi, Shoji and Dorothy's daughter, floats to the stage on a magic carpet in her "Arabian Nights" number.

Rows of tour buses are reflected in the theater facade. It's not unusual to see more than a dozen buses in front of Shoji's theater for both matinee and evening performances.

The patriotic finale of the show brings the audience to its feet and is videotaped for later television and tape release.

SHOJI TABUCHI

A mile or so down the Shepherd of the Hills Expressway from Ray Stevens' theater stands Shoji Tabuchi's purple neon pleasure palace, a theater whose facade and interior design, directly influenced by the sumptuous movie palaces of the 1930s, says, "Too much is not enough." It also houses the most extravagant—and most famous—restrooms west of the Mississippi. Tourists and bus tours come from all states to marvel at the decor and to fill the 2,000-seat theater to see Shoji Tabuchi, the Osaka-born country fiddle player who has put his own spin on Western swing and the "Orange Blossom Special."

Twice a day, six days a week, Shoji and his wife, Dorothy, put on a show that mixes his country music with her '50s sock hop/soda shoppe/Broadway pop song and dance numbers.

He makes fun of his own accent: "I'm from Louisiana also," he says after a Cajun number. "That's why I have this accent—northern Louisiana." Then he introduces his orchestra: "Everyone on the bandstand has a degree in music," he comments. "Only one up here with no music degree is . . . me." Appreciative laughter comes from the audience. "I got a degree in business," he muses.

Dorothy Tabuchi, producer and MC, directs, sings, and dances in skits: Broadway production numbers that include roller skaters, a motorcycle, big, moving sets, and more neon. No special effect is ignored in these extravagant production numbers. "That's theatrical smoke and fog, folks—it is non-toxic and acid free," says a voice before the lasers are turned on.

Modelled after a 1930s movie palace, Shoji's neon-decked theater seats 2,000 people and houses two celebrated bathrooms and extravagant gift shops.

Shoji Tabuchi was roped into American country music by Roy Acuff and the Smoky Mountain Boys band when he heard them play in Osaka. Osaka's loss is Branson's gain.

76 MUSIC HALL

It's all there under one roof, a complete entertainment complex – a musical bonanza. The 76 Music Hall is an intimate theater that hosts four different shows every day. The Music Hall itself is inside a mall, a former Wal-Mart building, which the owners converted into an indoor entertainment complex in the late '80s. Besides live music shows, it houses the busiest Bonanza restaurant in the chain, a 36-hole miniature golf course, a video arcade, and gift shops.

One can catch The Brumley Show (called by many "the best little music show in town") at 10 a.m., then do lunch at Bonanza, just down the hall. At 1:30, it's Down Home Country, followed at 4 p.m. by the Texas Gold Miners. Ready for a break? There's still shopping and dinner before The Memory Makers musical journey through time begins at 8 p.m.

During the evening show, The Memory Makers present The Sounds of Time, music and dancing from the 1940s to the '90s. Here, Diana Houseman and Splinter Middleton sing "Unforgettable."

At the Brumley Music Show, Miss Jeanie Dee sings to an enthusiastic crowd. The Brumley Show features Tom Brumley, renowned steel guitarist, his sons Todd and Tommy, and many gospel numbers by his father, Albert E. Brumley Sr., author of such classics as "I'll Fly Away" and "Turn Your Radio On."

Below.
Down Home Country Music Show gets its audience into the Western swing of things.

Below right.
The Texas Gold Miners give a peppy performance, singing, clogging, fiddle-playing, and doing impersonations.

CRISTY LANE

Cristy Lane's theater, with its distinctive arched facade featuring a portrait of the recording star, showcases Cristy and her smooth singing. Cristy achieved impressive success in the 1970s without the publicity machine of a major label behind her. Cristy and her husband, Lee Stoller, hand-built her career, from East Peoria housewife to international recording star. She made substantial record sales through late-night television commercials. She won fans on her own, recording on her own independent label. She achieved star status when she was named "New Vocalist of the Year" in 1979 by the Academy of Country Music. At that point United Artists Records signed her. She found the one song she had been looking for, and "One Day at a Time" became the keystone of her best-selling gospel album.

Also performing at Cristy Lane's are other nationally-known acts such as Ferlin ("On the Wings of a Dove") Husky and Vern Gosdin.

Cristy Lane bought the theater, formerly the Starlite Theatre Company, in 1989 from Chisai Childs. It was here that Chisai, the first woman emcee in Branson, brought her own brand of production to Branson from her first theater, the Grapevine (Texas) Opry.

THE BRASCHLER MUSIC SHOW

The Braschler Quartet first played the Branson area on Indian Point south of Silver Dollar City in 1984. They moved to their present location, the 715-seat Music Land USA on Gretna Road the following year. They changed their name to The Braschler Music Show to better describe the variety of entertainment they present. Originally a gospel quartet, they still include plenty of gospel in their show, but also play current country hits and grand old standards, and feature vigorous playing of a variety of instruments, including saxophone. In 1985 the Braschlers had a hit record, "The Antioch Church Choir," a touching story of an old man who wanted to sing in the choir but couldn't get in. He did, finally, find a choir that would let him sing . . . in heaven.

The Braschlers seem to be thriving by virtue of musicianship and lively, well-timed comedy in the new Branson mix, which increasingly features stars of the national media. Not only is the theater frequently sold out, but their tours to adjoining states during the winter season are also frequently sold out a season in advance. The Braschlers might play the

Wellington, Kansas, high school auditorium on a snowy Tuesday in February. Many members of that audience will then travel to Branson the following summer to spend an evening at The Braschler Music Show.

Every song is crisply played and sung and applauded by the audience. Every skit is as broad and hilarious as family vaudeville in its prime. The Braschlers' comedian, Terry Sanders, otherwise known as Homer Lee, the janitor, who has been featured on "HeeHaw," has created many raucous characters, among them Grandma Braschler. The repartee between Cliff Braschler and Grandma Braschler is fast and funny, as Cliff announces intermission and shows examples of *everything* they sell at the souvenir stand. ("Let 'er rip, tater chip," chirps Grandma as they toss a frisbee into the audience.) It's worth the price of admission. Watch out when Great Aunt Eunice shuffles in . . . .

"Can we talk?" Terry Sanders does an uncanny Joan Rivers impersonation. A local boy made good and a veteran of "HeeHaw," Terry performs at Shad and Mollie Heller's original Toby Show at Silver Dollar City and cracks up the crowd at the Braschlers'.

The Braschlers are proud of the newest member of the show, 19-year-old Justin Bertoldi, who plays mandolin, fiddle, and guitar.

Familiar music performed in a spirited style forms the core of this Branson show. Cliff Braschler (on left) is the founder and emcee of the Braschler Music Show.

MEL TILLIS

Mel Tillis's numerous major achievements in the field of country music include, but are not limited to, 1976 CMA Entertainer of the Year, huge record sales, writer of hit songs for himself and others ("Detroit City" for Bobby Bare, "Ruby, Don't Take Your Love to Town" for Kenny Rogers, and many more), and, of all things, television talk show guest–fairly unusual for someone with a stutter. "I been stutterin' . . . all my life–thirty years p-p-p-professionally." As audiences and host hang on every word, you realize that he's turned that stutter, the curse of his childhood, into an asset.

Like a number of Branson luminaries, Mel found Branson through Roy Clark's open door at the Celebrity Theatre. After playing dates there, he leased the Ozark Theatre after Shoji Tabuchi moved into his new place in 1990. Mel played there for two seasons before moving to the 2,100-seat Mel Tillis Theater, where he played for another two seasons, hosting live broadcast segments of the Jerry Lewis Muscular Dystrophy telethon in 1993.

Mel's bringing Broadway to Branson, as his spiffy brochure announces. He's got dancers, special effects, and a rain curtain. Marie Osmond sings there two days a week, and he occasionally turns host duties over to his daughter, Pam ("Queen of Denial") Tillis.

M-Mel's on the m-move. A man of restless energy and drive, Mel Tillis has announced plans to build a new theater with full television production facilities. He may be glad to live and sing in the same place, but Mel's no stranger to the road. Brenda Lee recalls touring with Mel in the middle '60s, before there were customized tour buses like these. "Mel would drive all night, so he'd want me to tell him stories to keep him awake, because I was a night owl, too. We'd travel those two-lane roads that went through God-knows-how-many little towns. It was great, because you got to see the world."

MUSICAL THEATERS

One permanent feature of the Branson entertainment landscape is change. Here the phrase "musical theaters" can have a double meaning. There's music played inside, all right, but the players and the buildings are often swapped around. When Jim Stafford moved to the former Lowe's Country Music Theatre, John Davidson took over his place. When Chisai Childs came to town from Grapevine, Texas, she produced her own shows and introduced new players to the scene (one of them was the second Japanese fiddle player in town, Shoji Tabuchi, now glitzing and glowing in his own place down the road) at the then Starlite Theatre—now the Cristy Lane Theatre ("One Day at a Time" has kept her there for five years). When the Plummer Family decided to retire, they sold their theater to Moe Bandy. Also, if you look closely, you may begin to recognize musicians you've seen before, since some play a morning show at one theater and a matinee or evening show at another theater. A few may even play after hours at restaurants or lounges around town.

The list of changes (and it is long) is for historians and makers of board games. Unlike the "musical chairs" game of childhood, however, the number of theaters in Branson is not diminishing and the number of players seems to be growing. But the moveable stars and migrating players keep the stages looking fresh. Country music troubadours who find a venue in Branson often return, some for a week, some for a season, some for a place of their own.

The Ozark Theater was originally built to house Mark Trimble's vintage automobile collection. After the collection was sold, the building was remodelled, and in 1989 it became Shoji's first theater. The following year, Mel Tillis leased it for two seasons before moving to a 2,100-seat space on Highway 65. Willie Nelson took it for 1992, sharing headliner duties with Merle Haggard. In 1993, Loretta Lynn leased it, but her run was cut short by her husband Mooney's serious illness. Charley Pride's appearances were so satisfying to both Charley and his loyal fans that he announced plans to build his own 1,999-seat theater in Branson. Significantly, Charley Pride's theater will be the first country music venue to open in Branson since Moe Bandy opened in 1991.

In the 1980s and into the early '90s there shone a country sun in Branson's entertainment firmament. National television and recording stars such as Roy Clark, Mickey Gilley, Moe Bandy, Mel Tillis, and Ray Stevens came. Independent entertainers who had shone brightly without the help of a major label, like Boxcar Willie, and in that special sky of late-night television, like Cristy Lane, came. A lot of live music shows sprang up on 76 west of its intersection with 165. A number of theaters changed hands, were remodeled, and expanded. A few of the acts from the 1970s, like Bob Mabe and The Plummer Family, and early '80s, like The Lowes, retired. The two original acts, Presleys' and Baldknobbers, just kept getting bigger and better.

Innovations marked this era. Chisai Childs and others took the clogs off the dancers and added lots of costume changes and a revolving stage, as well as special Christmas and New Year's shows. Branson shows began to integrate bits and pieces from Broadway musicals and Vegas-style vaudeville skits, a trend that eventually culminated in pink smoke, rain curtains, and laser lights in some formerly all country acts like Shoji Tabuchi and Mel Tillis.

But for the most part, the '80s saw many pure country acts take root in Branson, acts that primarily consisted of solid, traditional country singing and playing, a little gospel, and old fashioned, crack-up corny humor—a staple from tent shows to vaudeville to early television variety shows. These acts did add modern sound systems, theatrical lighting, and computers to run the box office. The duo of girl backup singers changed their costumes a little more often than before, too.

While Branson went humming along, writers for the *New York Times* penned obituaries for the country music business and the Nashville Sound in 1985 as record sales "plummeted." Maybe in the process of canning country, a lot of the farm-fresh flavor had gotten lost. The writers had forgotten that there was a whole world of country music, like bluegrass festivals, honky-tonk bars, and stars touring state fairs, that had little to do with Music Row. Branson was a big part of that world, and it continued to thrive, even as some prematurely mourned country music's "passing."

The oldest and most traditional entertainment in America is country music. It is a music about individualism, played and sung by individualists, self-reliant entrepreneurs like Roy Clark. In a frontier kind of way they came to Branson and took the music business into their own hands. Most of the theaters built during this period are either owned outright or in partnership by the performers whose names shine in neon on their marquees.

The hegemony of country ended in the early '90s with the arrival of Andy Williams and the advent of big, architect-

designed palaces such as those of Wayne Newton, Tony Orlando, and Bobby Vinton. Branson became a refuge or sanctuary for entertainers and entrepreneurs fed up with the changes that the corporatization of the arts and entertainment underwent in the 1980s. Sony acquired Columbia; English and German firms swallowed up newspaper publishing. Young MBAs with Arab money hatched entertainment schemes. Meanwhile, Branson continued to entertain and do business in its own entrepreneurial, down-home, Main Street USA way.

The musical theaters game continues in Branson. The year after this photo was taken, Jim Stafford bought the Lowe's Theater next door and sold his to John Davidson. The Lowe Sisters opened their theater in 1983. As their marquee shows, they frequently brought national acts to Branson. Loretta Lynn performed as many as 125 dates a year there. Others included Ricky Skaggs, Bill Monroe, Porter Wagoner, and Johnny Rodriguez.

Life on the road can be exciting and live performances sell records, but in time it can prove to be tiresome. There's wear and tear on more than just the tires.

Branson shows forever seek fresh combinations of talent. Don't expect all the marquees to read the same the next time you come to town.

The hills are alive with the sound of construction.
Branson, however, has a program of reforestation.
It seems probable that much of the natural character
of the area will be preserved by planning and because
a lot of publicly owned park land remains.

BOOMTOWN BRANSON

Not every doodle on a cocktail napkin becomes an architect's rendering, and not every blueprint becomes a building. But if even a fraction of the announced projects are realized, Branson will indeed become an international tourist mecca. Serious people with serious money stand behind many of the developments slated for the Shepherd of the Hills Country. This book looks at Branson through a Nikon lens, not a crystal ball. It's anybody's guess where it will all end, but even the most pessimistic viewer must allow that at this point Branson's future certainly does glow.

Boomtowns are a well-known feature of the Old West. When the railroad came, or gold or oil was discovered, the most exciting part of a business cycle, rapid and continuous economic activity, began. In many cases, such booms were followed by busts when the resources ran out or the new town became overbuilt.

Branson has experienced several such booms in the past. The coming of the White River Line, the cutting of the virgin timber, and the building of the dams all quickened the town's economic pulse for a time. The current entertainment boom *may* be somewhat less subject to bust:

The global tourist industry is now the world's biggest

For years 76 Country Boulevard was the preferred address of commercial development. Today numerous access roads provide attractive alternatives for theaters, shops, restaurants, and motels. They all feed into 76, relieving congestion on the clogged main artery.

employer; one out of every fifteen workers across the planet spends the day transporting, feeding, housing, herding, cosseting, or amusing tourists. ("The End of Jobs," Richard J. Barnet, senior fellow at the Institute for Policy Studies, Washington, DC, in *Harpers* magazine, September 1993.)

The kind of family oriented entertainment Branson has always provided is, in fact, in precious short supply worldwide, having been judged by most media gurus as too unhip and uncommercial. If Branson remains true to its image, which it seems to be doing unerringly, many more neon dreams will be making that perilous journey from drawing board to shining reality.

NEW TECHNOLOGY

The ear-splitting squawk of microphone feedback is only a memory today in Branson. All the theaters have invested in the latest technology of sound and lighting. The music is produced the old fashioned way, with trained human larynx and hand held bow, but the vibrations are captured, mixed,and sent out to all parts of the theater with the help of million dollar sound systems operated by skilled technicians. Exciting and expressive lighting effects are also constantly being added.

The fact that many of Branson's performers have been television celebrities may explain the extensive and artful use of in-show videos. This ability to show close-ups of the performance adds an intimate dimension to even the largest auditorium.

The most significant and newest technological trend is the capacity of some of Branson's theaters to produce satellite television broadcasts. The segments of national telethons originating in Branson are technically indistinguishable from programming originating in the media centers of Los Angeles and New York. Firms now headquartered in Branson have the ability to make video and audio productions that can compete in the international marketplace. The Americana Television Network, which originates in Branson, is now on cable, and shows great promise. Other television and recording firms have also announced plans to open offices in Branson, and Branson's exploding television industry has come as a shock to media moguls.

Sound board at Bobby Vinton's Blue Velvet Theatre.

Branson Teleproductions not only has editing and tape duplication facilities, but it also has two semi-truck-sized mobile television studios.

Remember, however, that in the 1950s Red Foley's "Ozark Jubilee" originated from nearby Springfield, which was, at the time, the third largest originator of live programming in the United States. Branson may emerge not only as a live performance capital, but also as a center for all kinds of media production.

RAY STEVENS THEATRE

On the east slope of Dewey Bald stands the Ray Stevens Theatre. Inside, twice a day, six days a week, Ray plays. That's what his show is about: play. Plays on words; play that we all did in the sandbox era of our lives; play about life and characters that is so devastatingly accurate it's funny. With his raucous support system of pink aliens, a bald brother, the French Fried Far Out Legion Band, a mincing pirate, and nearly endless stories of colorful relatives providing source material, Ray packs two hours of songs and stories that surprise, titillate, and entertain. You know you've been to a show after you've seen Ray perform.

Now that he is cruising the stratospheric heights of satellite television, the question is: "Will Ray, now one of the most successful marketers of home video, stay to satisfy Branson's demand for his absolutely out-of-this- (or any other) world, pun-full, playful, pungent humor with never a rancorous, rancid tone, or will he take to the road again?" Whatever he decides, there will always be an audience for him in Branson.

Forever a sailor on the endless seas of the American sense of humor, Ray charted his own course from the beginning, and smelled the breeze. We become passengers on his talent from point of departure to destination. Buy a ticket and you'll see some sights, splashed along the way by some salty spray. It's exotic and familiar, and for two hours Ray Stevens is your Captain Ahab, the Georgian on a great adventure. You'll return to see home as you've never seen it before. Ray has taken you on the most exotic cruise of all: around the block in your own hometown.

Left. Clyde the Purple Neon Camel sets the desert theme of Ray's theater.

Left below. The French Fried Far Out Legion Band joins in the general silliness as they cluck a new version of "In the Mood."

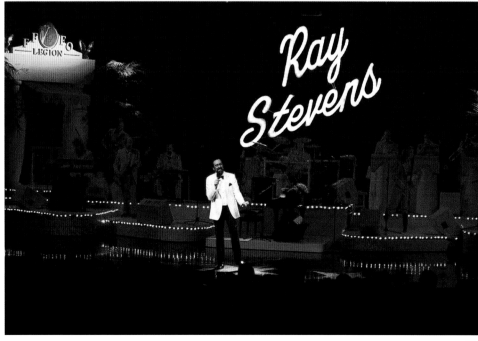

JIM STAFFORD

There's an amazing quality to the Jim Stafford show. First of all, there is Stafford himself. His boyish good looks belie a wicked sense of humor. Sometimes Jim spins a web of fantasy that glistens in the morning dew. Once the audience is entrapped he shows us the spider or snake or swamp witch. Then it gets a little dangerous. The smiles turn to nervous titters and finally to belly laughs when the realization comes that one has been caught in the magic spell of a great illusionist. It's solid Southern sorcery, all the more entertaining when the trap has been sprung by a charming, guitar-picking genius of country comedy.

This illusion isn't all verbal either. Jim and his cast are, in reality, superb musicians. But the naughtiness factor always creeps in. Sometimes just when the song sounds about as beautiful as it has ever been played—here come those cosmic, comic rays from outer Stafford space. ZAP . . . you're had. Ray Stevens is another out-of-this-world comedian whose flying saucer hovers in Southern skies, but his world-beyond-this-world derives its fantasy from rural community life. Jim's blast-off point is the puzzling and wonderous experiences individuals have—like having a chihuahua for a pet, or babies

The facade of Jim Stafford's theater pays homage to the American movie palace of yesteryear. It was here that the late, great Conway Twitty played his last date, June 4, 1993.

and all the baby-ness that comes with them. Jim's new son, Sheaffer James, at six months of age already a veteran Branson performer, frequently helps his father out with "The Little Kids' Song."

"Gimme that old soft shoe." Stafford's show displays a compendium of the arts of the American stage, delightfully worked and skillfully executed.

*The players and singers
in Stafford's cast are deft,
dapper, and personable.*

ANDY WILLIAMS MOON RIVER THEATRE

If you watched variety TV in the late sixties and early seventies you probably ran across "The Andy Williams Show." Now Mr. Williams has alighted in Branson, along with his old friend Cookie Bear, new friend juggler Philip Wellford, and a cast of singers and dancers to continue his brand of all-American entertainment. His almost constantly packed houses indicate that the family variety show form of entertainment continues to have a large and diverse audience, a fact the media moguls often underestimate.

In 1991, Andy's brother, Don Williams, who is Ray Stevens' manager, invited Andy to visit Ray's new theater. By his own account, only two days later Andy made the decision to pack up and move his operation to this Ozark town for good, drawn like so many before him by the opportunity to design and present a show exactly as he wants it while living at home. The Moon River Theatre opened on May 1, 1992.

Andy Williams' Moon River Theatre is, perhaps, the most architecturally distinctive theater on 76 Country Boulevard.

Impressed by the dramatic highway cuts made through the Ozark mountains, Williams engaged Springfield architect Warren Bates and the Larson Company, a firm that designs, fabricates, and constructs artificial environments, to realize his vision. They replicated in concrete the limestone strata which flank these mountain roads, even to the drilling scars, mineral stains, lichens, and fungus. In front of this rocky fortress flows "Moon River." The interior of the lobby is equally distinctive with original art works by de Kooning, Lipschitz, and Henry Moore, as well as Navajo rugs from Williams' collection.

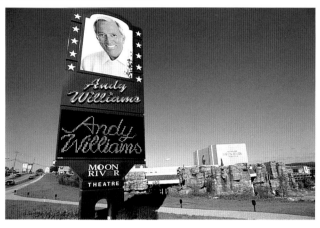

A post-matinee crowd strolls across Moon River.

THE OSMOND FAMILY THEATER

At the junction of 76 Country Boulevard and Highway 165 stands The Osmond Family Theater, where five of the Osmond Brothers, Alan, Wayne, Merrill, Jay, and Jimmy, put on two shows daily for busloads of still-avid fans. Once the darlings of "The Andy Williams Show," today they do a novelty version of their backup to "Moon River," sans Mr. Williams. The format of the show is variety, and when every member of a large family plays, sings, and dances, the permutations are astronomical. Apparently no Osmond lacks musical talent. Virtually all of them are seasoned performers on at least half a dozen instruments. To top it off, "The Second Generation" is coming on strong, attracting a second generation of fans for this indefatigable family.

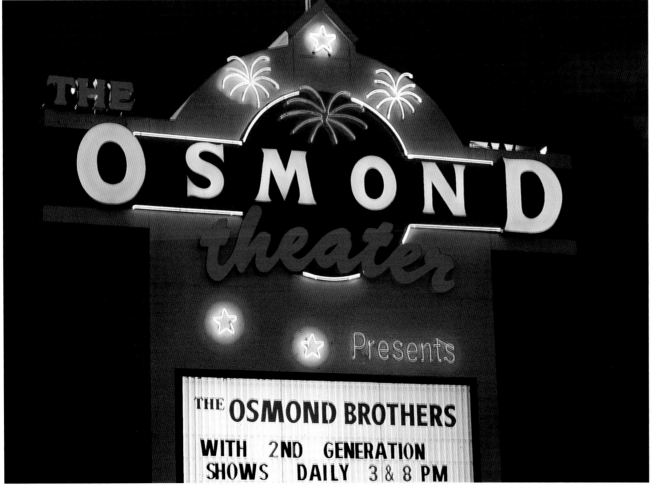

Once the home of the Bob-o-Links Country Hoe-down, one of the early shows on 76, The Osmond Family Theater has been remodelled and updated to accommodate the family and their fans.

Multi-colored flashing neon fireworks light up The Osmond Family Theater sign near the junction of 76 Country Boulevard and Highway 165.

119

JOHN DAVIDSON

During the Christmas season of 1992 John Davidson, who was then doing matinee shows at Jim Stafford's theater, commented to a reporter, "We will see how it goes for next year. A lot of people are talking about a lot of exciting things." The exciting thing for him was buying Jim's theater and opening his own show in the 1993 season.

He is a public-spirited performer, lending his talents to local and national causes. When Wayne Newton produced the Flood Relief telethon at his Branson theater, John Davidson undertook the formidable task of tying all those taped and live segments together. His easygoing temperament made the challenging task of emcee seem easy.

Located between Jim Stafford's and Boxcar Willie's establishments is John Davidson's theater, which sports some snazzy neon embellishments.

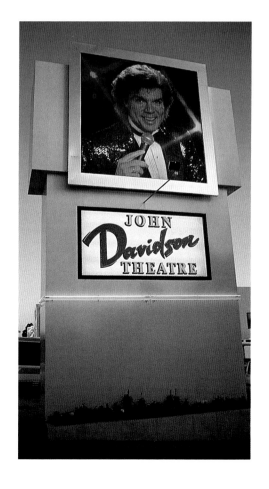

Davidson is a well-known television personality who brings an intimate style to his performances. Every lady in the audience feels that he sings especially to her. The charming host of several TV shows, "That's Incredible" and "The John Davidson Show," to name only a couple, he has also starred in Broadway productions and nightclubs in Lake Tahoe, Las Vegas, and Reno. He has a low-key, amiable personality, and his fans respond warmly to it.

Davidson remodelled his theater, removing some seats and expanding the stage to give him greater access to his audience.

THE GRAND PALACE

The name says it all: it is grand. The largest theater in Branson, its presence is such that it can be seen from across the river, through the trees. A resplendent edifice built in an antebellum Southern plantation style, The Grand Palace features a colonnaded front entrance, a custom designed brass and crystal chandelier, and a sweeping double staircase rising to the second floor.

From its inception, The Grand Palace was intended to augment the Branson entertainment scene. Other Branson theaters are single-star showcases with an occasional visiting celebrity. The Grand Palace was designed to be a rotating venue for current top country stars. Today, Louise Mandrell and Glen Campbell perform the host duties, while other major stars shine at the Palace every week. Hot new performers like Dwight Yoakam, Brooks and Dunn, and Mark Chesnutt play the Palace Super Sundays. Billy Ray Cyrus, who also did a Sunday at the Palace, didn't even seem to mind that almost every other show in town has a comic version of "Achy Breaky Heart." Not everyone who comes is country, however. Gladys Knight, Doc Severinsen, Bill Cosby, and The Captain and Tenille add spice to the Palace's already varied entertainment menu.

Designed in an antebellum Southern mansion style, the reception area of the Palace fronts the huge auditorium.

The Grand Palace, a Silver Dollar City and Kenny Rogers property, sits near the mid-point of 76 Country Boulevard. The 4,000-seat theater, the largest in Branson, houses full television production capabilities. Beyond the Palace, across Lake Taneycomo in the green hills, one can see the College of the Ozarks.

That little whirlwind up there on that great big stage singing, dancing (usually both at the same time), and playing a bunch of instruments is Louise Mandrell. The resident hostess of The Grand Palace is, it has been noted, a hard act to follow.

The signature grand piano in the lobby has been signed by visiting and resident stars.

During performances four huge television screens above the stage give the audience close-ups of the acts or pre-recorded videos relating to what's happening on stage. The Grand Palace also has full television production and broadcasting facilities and a recording studio. Several television specials have already been produced there. The Grand Palace is owned and operated by Silver Dollar City in partnership with Kenny Rogers.

The keel has also been laid (by Kenny Rogers, as a matter of fact) on a sort of Grand Palace that floats: a paddlewheeler on Table Rock Lake, currently under construction, which will have—what else?—live music on its cruises. Despite Kenny Rogers' hit song "The Gambler," the deck is stacked against gambling here, or for that matter, any place else in Branson. The die was cast long ago for clean living and family entertainment in the Shepherd of the Hills country.

The Herschend brothers, Pete and Jack, who own Silver Dollar City, decided on the Grand leap into contemporary entertainment after developing Dollywood at Pigeon Forge, Tennessee, in partnership with Dolly Parton. They announced their plans in the fall of 1990, began Palace construction in 1991, and opened the doors to an awestruck public on May 1, 1992. In October of that year The Grand Palace was named "Venue of the Year" by the Country Music Association.

Glen Campbell, the boy from Delight, Arkansas, has followed a long road to reach Branson as resident host of The Grand Palace. He's been pickin' and strummin' (in Los Angeles studios) since the early 1950s, hit the charts with "Gentle on My Mind," and collected gold singles with a couple of Jimmy Webb songs, "Galveston" and "By the Time I Get to Phoenix."

Four video screens surround the stage, giving all sections of the audience close-ups of the performance.

JOHNNY CASH

"Hello. I'm Johnny Cash and I play music." The famous bass rumbled through the Wayne Newton Theatre as Johnny and his wife, June Carter Cash, opened to a standing ovation.

Johnny wasn't kidding–they play music (no lasers, no dancers, no neon). The couple fill two hours with so many songs we all know . . . songs they've written, songs they've sung . . . that there's no time for more. He fronts a tight, hard-driving band with a distinctive style of story-telling music that defies

electricity to power the hamlets they hail from. Instead, they did live radio and television, Fourth of July celebrations, and a host of other congenial gatherings in rural and small-town America.

Johnny, June, the Carter Family, and son John Carter Cash performed eight weeks at the Wayne Newton Theatre during their first season in Branson.

June, her daughter Rosey, and her sisters, Helen and Anita, members of the legendary Carter Family, give the show a righteous foil to the Man in Black's powerful anthems of the human condition. Their rendition of "The Church in the Wildwood" is inspiring. In this deceptively simple song, they demonstrate marvelous possibilities in harmony and melody, because everything simple becomes complicated, rich, and exciting, if it is done right.

classification–he's in the Rock and Roll, Country Music, and Songwriters' Halls of Fame.

June Carter Cash, incidentally, can tell a story in such a way that if Mark Twain were in the audience he'd be writing it down . . . word for word. "We did work and sing all over these Ozark hills with Mother Maybelle," she says, launching into a story of the worst snowstorm she'd ever seen, about 1950, when they ran out of gas trying to get from Branson to Springfield on a cold winter night to appear the next morning on "Red Foley's Ozark Jubilee" television show. "Chester flagged down a pig truck." Her fast-paced story of the too-fast tow sounds fanciful, made-up, until you find out that Chet Atkins was traveling with the Carter Family at the time and tells the same story. This was before country musicians played 3,000-seat, air-conditioned palaces with sound systems that draw enough

As June says, "We just come in with our guitars and good looks and push it on through."

WAYNE NEWTON THEATRE

The Wayne Newton Theater is located along the Shepherd of the Hills Expressway a couple of miles off 76 Country Boulevard. Though it is not on 76, it is visible from practically every part of the highway and from Dewey Bald and almost every other ridgetop for miles around. Painted bright white, it shines out from the green hills and brown construction sites that surround it.

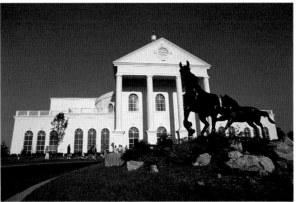

Wayne's showmanship touches every moment of the show, from the laser-lit landing of a flying saucer piloted by a pink alien who delivers Wayne to the top of a curved white staircase, to the lightning-thunder-rain-curtain and laser effects that accompany Wayne's finale, "MacArthur Park." No intermission in this show . . . Wayne builds up steam and keeps the show rolling for two packed hours.

The bronze Arabians in front of the Wayne Newton Theatre are a favorite photo background for his fans. The 78,000-square-foot, Virginian-style theater seats 3,000.

It's never exactly the same show, either. He gets the feel of the audience with instincts finely honed during his decades of live performing and swings into the music he knows they will love the most. Sometimes, when he's decided his course, it's just Wayne and his rhythm section, as the orchestra searches through their charts. He's got a real orchestra, too, twenty-nine pieces (trumpets, trombones, saxophones – four each – a string section, French horn, harp, and a white grand piano), plus five backup singers. It's a big stage, in a big theater (3,000 seats), but if the power ever goes the band will fill the hall, even without its high tech amplification system.

The lobby showcases Wayne's 1929 Dusenberg, formerly owned by Howard Hughes, and silver-laden show saddles for his prized Arabians.

The stage is full of instruments that Wayne will play with a repertoire that includes, but is not limited to, country-western, swing, Top 40, rock 'n roll, Broadway show tunes, and gospel. The arrangements are all tailored to Wayne's knock-'em-dead style. As Wayne himself has said, "People may leave one of my shows disliking Wayne Newton, but they've never walked out saying, 'He didn't work hard for us' or 'He didn't give us our money's worth.'"

Wayne pulls out all the stops for his audience. His is the largest stage in Branson, and he covers every foot of it during his animated performances. Devoted fans, called Wayniacs, come from everywhere, often attending his show several times during a single visit to Branson.

TONY ORLANDO YELLOW RIBBON MUSIC THEATER

Tony Orlando Yellow Ribbon Music Theater opened on July 4, 1993. It's a tasteful, architect-designed structure with comfortable seating, a great lighting system, and enough slope in the floor to allow a good view from every seat in the house. It is a truly elegant venue.

Tony's son, Jon, is the host who greets the bus tours, congratulates anniversary celebrants, and after a few jokes asks, "Ready for my Dad?"

"Bring him out!" people holler, and the show is on. Tony himself has an infectious sense of humor. Don't sit in the front row if you don't want to be his new best friend and possibly end up on stage doing "The Beer Barrel Polka" with him.

Even at a mid-week matinee, Tony pours it on. He rolls up his sleeves, unbuttons his collar, and sets about entertaining. He talks to his audience, he sings

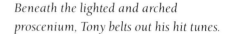

to them, he hustles a man named Larry up on to the stage to sing and dance with him. Even after he lets Larry go, he talks to him or about him occasionally from the stage. Tony is generous with his stage, too. He introduces Robbie Clark, a parking lot attendant who happens to play a mean country fiddle. When Robbie gets a standing ovation, Tony asks, "Anything else I can do for you, Robbie?" "How 'bout a level parking lot?" Everyone who has hiked up the hill from a lower lot laughs.

A vaulted skylight runs the length of the lobby. Its mirrored end reflects the stained glass yellow ribbon mounted above the main entrance, the image for which the theater is named.

Beneath the lighted and arched proscenium, Tony belts out his hit tunes.

After his 1970s hit records and his CBS variety show, Tony did Broadway, portraying the life of P.T. Barnum on stage. He's brought that high style Broadway production to Branson in an entrancing circus number in which he recreates his role as P(hineas) T(aylor) Barnum. Tony is as much a showman as Barnum was, and as circus posters descend behind the band, a man on stilts, clowns, a juggler, and Ringmaster Tony take over the stage and our imaginations.

P.T. Barnum comes to Branson, as Tony recreates his Broadway role as the legendary ringmaster.

FIVE STAR THEATRE
THE BEROSINI & VANBURCH SHOW

In an age of overdone digital mystifications on television and splashy special effects in movies, there is still real magic in live performance. Two hours pass in a flash ("did we really see the show—or was it another amazing illusion?") with the Five Star Theatre's combination of hi-jinxing orangutans, I-can't-believe-my-eyes illusions, and the most energetic dance numbers this side of Broadway.

Bobby Berosini, who hails from the wooded slopes of Czechoslovakia, credibly sells himself as a transplanted hillbilly when he does a yodelling number. Country is country, no matter what country it's from, and Branson has always welcomed those with a hillbilly heart. Orangutans are funny and almost frighteningly human at the same time just sitting there looking at you. When they start interacting with Bobby, you wonder who is entertaining whom. Bobby seems to end up as the brunt of most of their schtick. Maybe the act should be called "The Orangutan Troupe and Their Trained Human."

"They love people. As soon as they get onstage and see the crowd of smiling people, they give a great performance. It's because they have fun."

The song may be in Czechoslovakian, but the sentiments (and the yodel) are definitely country.

Kirby VanBurch doesn't make you laugh. He presents a spectacle of an altogether different order – mystery. You can hear the jaws drop in the eighteenth row when, in a puff of smoke, a tiger appears in an empty cage. Motorcycles, girls, huge snakes, white ducks: they appear, disappear, and reappear. They do things that any sensible person knows cannot be done. As the kids leave they all ask: "How did he do that?" and "When can we come back?"

Kirby VanBurch looks into the eye of a leopard that has just appeared in the cage.

BOBBY VINTON'S BLUE VELVET THEATRE

"Branson is like America used to be," Bobby Vinton explained in a live interview with Katie Couric of "The Today Show" on the opening day of his Branson showcase. He touted the virtues of this small Ozark town with its big-time opportunities in interviews on television talk shows and in magazine articles for months before his grand opening.

He's a decisive man: a two-day stint at Roy Clark's Celebrity Theatre in October 1992 resulted in the opening of a 2,000-seat "Vinton Theatre" in the center of action on 76 Country Boulevard in September 1993. While many theaters are partnerships, Vinton owns every blue tile and velvet curtain himself.

In spite of the size of his theater, Bobby maintains an intimate, cabaret-like atmosphere in his show. He charts new territory in meeting his audience. While many performers keep to the first five or ten rows, he sings his way to the back, having his picture taken, urging anniversary couples to dance as he sings, "How we danced on the night we were wed." Many do, and each aisle has at least one couple waltzing as he sings. You get the feeling that romances are rekindled at his show and that couples who danced in the aisles leave holding hands.

Younger members of the audience have rediscovered Vinton's music. As he himself said: "I'm so far out, I'm in." Hipster David Lynch lavishly and effectively used Vinton's rich harmonics in the movie score for *Blue Velvet*, and the same song became a number one hit in England in 1993. As he runs through his long string of hits, it suddenly dawns on you that you've probably spent hours and hours listening to him over the years.

Just across the street from the Grand Palace stands Bobby Vinton's distinctive Blue Velvet Theatre.

*Although Bobby Vinton's
fame and fortune have
come from Top 40 hits,
his true passion is big
band standards. A highly
educated musician himself,
Vinton writes the arrangements
for this swinging orchestra.*

*The old Glenn Miller classics never sounded better
than when played by this troupe of dedicated pros.*

MORNING SHOWS

Ozark mornings, even in the heart of the summer, are frequently cool and delightful. Early explorers spoke of the region's "salubrious" climate . . . an old word meaning healthful. For many visitors the morning shows are salubrious – starting the day with a song and a laugh, and at a few revues, a cup of coffee and a pastry or even a full breakfast. As the fog burns out of the valleys, these effervescent entertainments lift the audiences' spirits.

*Below and **right.** Some lucky Branson visitor may start the day with a very personal song from Barbara Fairchild ("The Teddy Bear Song.")*

Buck Trent, a banjo picker's banjo picker, can also tell a great story.

Ferlin Husky will wake you up with his repertoire of the hits he made famous.

Jennifer in the Morning.

In most of the Branson area, plywood and paint billboards belong to a bygone era. Costly creations of custom-designed, backlit plastic or neon dominate the new age of signage.

A theme song for Branson might begin, "What's old is new, and what's new was once in." Country themes that were played here after they had been lost or forgotten elsewhere lie at the core of Branson's identity and success. Attracted to this dedication to traditional values and family audiences, performers of other genres of popular music have come to be part of this hometown atmosphere. They're packing them in, and the country acts are growing as well. The desire for a clean, well-lighted place to visit, a place that is safe, wholesome, and affordable, is not a fantasy at all. It's the Branson plan.

Branson is a neon dream. The lights shine multi-hued, as Branson diversifies with more colors of the entertainment spectrum.

Peter Engler, a north Arkansas wood carver, set up shop in
Silver Dollar City in 1963, instituting the City's support for
local crafts. In 1968, he expanded his operation to include
the Wilderness Clockworks in Reeds Spring, which served as
a retail outlet and training ground for other carvers.
In 1986, Engler renovated a 40,000-square foot warehouse
on 76 Country Boulevard into a replica of his grandfather's
Minnesota general store, named it Engler's Block, and invited
other craftspeople to exhibit and sell their works there.
Today it houses more than two dozen shops and galleries.
No longer limited to Ozark crafts, Engler's Block now features
jewelry, home decor, and specialty foods as well.

"Pump Boys and Dinettes" dances through a day
in the life of a country roadside diner.

Jennifer Wilson ("Jennifer in the Morning") has studied
many kinds of dance, but she invented "the Missouri Clog."

Kelly VanHoose and
Chris Gentile of the
Baldknobbers' Jamboree:
they sing, they dance,
they do eleven costume
changes in every show.

Broadway production numbers come to Branson via Las Vegas at the Five Star Theatre.

At the Down Home Country Show (76 Music Hall), intermission is preceded by a mirthful showing of selected souvenirs.

The phrase most Branson publicists and brochure writers use to describe the Branson variety show is "high energy." As with so many clichés, this one just happens to be accurate.

A member of the Blackwood Quartet serenades the front row.

The Norris Twins relax between performances.

The intrepid can make a big splash on Paradise Plunge at White Water.

Far left.
Between sets at the Boatworks Theater in Silver Dollar City.

Far left. *Tony Orlando.*

Left. *Bobby Vinton.*

Below left. *The Sons of the Pioneers, still corralling audiences and rolling out the records after 60 years.*

Left. Sonny Spencer of The Sons of the Pioneers.

Right. Glen Campbell.

Below right. Lori Locke with Greg and Scott Presley at Presleys' Jubilee.

WILDWOOD CHURCHES

A few minutes' drive from the bright lights lie wildwood churches, sawmill shacks, stonework cottages, and other architectural evidences of varied lives and times. Log cabins range in age from pioneer days to yesterday. Some are re-creations, some restorations. A few, like the Sycamore Log Church, are authentic to their location and still in use.

When Table Rock Dam was under construction in the 1950s, some primitive structures were rescued from the soon-to-be flooded White River bottoms and incorporated into Silver Dollar City. From the Wilderness Church's 1950 picture window Table Rock Lake can be seen today. College of the Ozarks preserves a one-room school, and Shepherd of the Hills Homestead has a frame church, both brought in from outside the area and lovingly restored. As one generation's memories are gradually replaced by another's, the Branson area is becoming a rich source of continuing nostalgia. From hand-hewn logs to the neon facades of steel-and-concrete music palaces, the record of America's many architectural modes in unusually evident.

Many long-time observers are cautiously optimistic that the Shepherd of the Hills Country will weather the current economic boom. The culture of an earlier America hangs like the morning mist over the hills and hollows of Branson. Likewise, the native landscape has proven extraordinarily resilient. The beauty of ballads and the expressiveness of spoken English remain the heritage of these old White River hills and all Americans.

The White River hills: view south from behind The Grand Palace.

Below left.
The Franz Family sings gospel in Mutton Hollow.

Below.
Sycamore Log Church.

The Wilderness Church in Silver Dollar City.

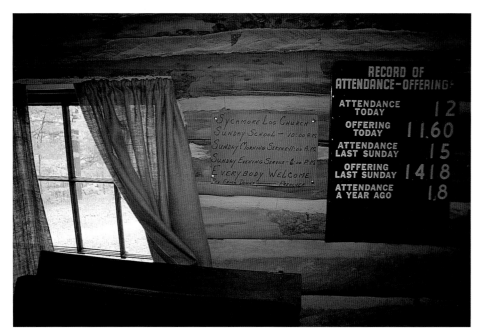

Viola Baptist Church.

ACKNOWLEDGEMENTS

To the many peformers and their staffs and all the people of Branson
whose openness and easy-going style made doing this book
so much fun: this book's for you.

SPECIAL THANKS TO

🍂 Ed Anderson, a joy to work with, he's a publisher
with a good heart and a good head.

🍂 Jim Hawkins — writers should be so lucky as to
have a literate designer and typesetter.

🍂 John Margolies, the poet in Kodachrome
of the American roadside.

🍂 Jim Jones

🍂 Stephanie Preninger

🍂 Vi and Lyn Asselin and The White River Historical Museum

🍂 Chlorene LaRue and Arlene Asher, who generously shared
their fine postcard collections with us

🍂 Linda Myers-Phinney

🍂 Lyons Memorial Library at College of the Ozarks

🍂 Springfield-Greene County Library System.

🍂 Nikon, Inc. Without my trusty Nikon F-4 I couldn't have done this book.
It's simply the best camera in the world.

🍂 Mrs. Patti Crystal for her staunch support through the years.

🍂 Strader and Ross Daniels Payton, who did a lot of intense research on the
recreational opportunities of Silver Dollar City and White Water.